On Tap

Mark McKay has a keen interest in the history of
Australian pubs and an even keener interest in the
beverages they serve. He works as a quarantine
sniffer-dog handler. Mark writes fiction,
and contributes to rock magazine *dB*.

On Tap

A cavalcade of trivia and tall stories

celebrating 200 years of the Australian pub

Mark McKay

ILLUSTRATIONS BY
STEPHEN EMERSON

Wakefield
Press

Wakefield Press
17 Rundle Street
Kent Town
South Australia 5071

First published 1999

Text copyright © Mark McKay, 1999
Illustrations copyright © Stephen Emerson, 1999

Designed by design BITE, Adelaide
Typeset by Clinton Ellicott, MoBros, Adelaide
Printed and bound by Hyde Park Press, Adelaide

National Library of Australia
Cataloguing-in-publication entry

McKay, Mark, 1963–   .
On tap: a cavalcade of trivia and tall stories celebrating
200 years of the Australian pub.

Includes index.
ISBN 1 86254 473 5.

1. Bars (Drinking establishments) – Australia – Miscellanea.
1. Bars (Drinking establishments) – Australia – Anecdotes.
1. Bars (Drinking establishments) – Australia – History.
I. Title.

647.9594.

ARTSA

Wakefield Press thanks Wirra Wirra Vineyards and Arts South Australia
for their continued support.

Contents

'There has always been a pub — hotel, inn or shanty or what you will — there should always be a pub, and there must always be one. All the wowsers in the Commonwealth might howl into my ears till they cure me of my deafness — or howl one stone deaf — but they won't howl that first, middle and last opinion out of my head.'

Henry Lawson, on the prohibition in force
in Leeton, New South Wales, 1916

Preface

In 200 years no other Australian institution has kept as true to its original ideals as the hotel – that is, to accommodate, feed and quench a thirst.

I have great personal memories of pubs. Memories of the late lamented Aurora Hotel in central Adelaide linger longer than the crack of the wrecking ball from which it fell. It was deliberately dark and dingy in an unfashionable quarter of town, inhabited by bikers and punks, the juke-box containing gems from The Jam, The Damned, The Clash and the Sex Pistols. Maybe it was just like the Star Hotel in Newcastle, which met a similar but more spectacular fate four years earlier, the same sort of anti-establishment clientele inhabiting a hotel thatwas run-down, but in exactly the way they liked it.

I have memories of the magnificent views of the Pacific Hotel in Yamba, NSW, or the Currumbin on the Gold Coast, the first sighting of 'Chloe', the beer after the game at the MCG Hotel, a steak at the Breakfast Creek Hotel, a cold beer after a long drive in Nyngan, meeting friends at such diverse places as the Marble Bar at the Sydney Hilton and the Racecourse Bar at the Highway Inn in Plympton. And it cheers me to know that people have been enjoying pubs in similar ways for the past two centuries. Now that's an institution.

An oasis in a dry country

Social developments over the last decade (drink-driving legislation among them) have meant that bottleshops are increasingly challenging hotels for the liquor dollar. But Australia had a bottle shop before it had a pub!

Governor Arthur Phillip's prohibition on the trading of liquor – the first of many new licensing laws in this country – ceased in 1792 when the Master of the *Royal Admiral*, Captain Bond, and his First Officer, Thomas Reibey, opened stores in Parramatta and Sydney to sell the cargo of their vessel, including the first beer imported into Australia. It was a dark brown bitter porter that soon ran out, solving – temporarily – the drunkenness problem it had caused.

Rums of varying strengths and other spirits were soon available, and they became a bargaining tool, even a currency. Convicts were paid in liquor. For the authorities, this was a cheap way of paying their captive labourers; for the convicts, the grog provided a temporary escape from their hardships.

This system of control through alcohol led to the overthrow of misguided and tyrannical Governor William Bligh in the Rum Rebellion of 1808. Bligh was arrested by Major George Johnston at the request of the officers of the New South Wales Corps as he had gained a monopoly on the trading and supply of rum.

Sly-grog shops flourished in the 1790s and Governor Hunter ordered the closure of several illegal public houses, believing them to be a 'public nuisance' due to their lack of regulation. Hunter issued Australia's first ten liquor licences for consumption on premises in April 1796. These cost the new licensees the tidy sum of £20 with sureties of £10 as well.

The records for the majority of these licences have been lost but it appears that one of the new licences was for the Mason's Arms in Parramatta, opened by a French–Jewish ticket-of-leave man named James Larra. On land owned by John Macarthur, Larra's single-roomed, wattle-and-daub hut was the first site leased in Parramatta. The inn was a successful business and was also known as the Free Mason's Arms, then the Freemason's Arms.

Extended in 1800, the Freemason's Arms was popular for its accommodation, attracting clientele mainly from Sydney, and winning a reputation as a private hotel for discerning guests rather than a public house. The site of Larra's original pub is now occupied by the Parramatta Court House, but the Woolpack Hotel across the road claims to operate under the same – Australia's oldest licence.

Governor Hunter hoped to reduce public drunkenness by granting a few licences to sell liquor. He was far too optimistic: social problems associated with alcohol abuse became widespread. A second wave of licences was issued in 1798 and in the following year Hunter placed a limit on the number of licences issued for each locality. Sly-grog shops continued to flourish, however, even after magistrates had issued fifteen more licences than the intended sixteen. Historians say that it

Woolpack Hotel, Parramatta, NSW

was around this time that Australia earned its reputation as a hard-drinking country.

In those days, a 'tavern' tended to be more raucous and less refined than an 'inn', as opposed to today's trend of renaming an estalishment as a tavern after refurbishment or renovation. Premises that existed to cater for travellers were called 'halfway houses' or 'staging-post inns' and were the brainchild of revolutionary Governor Lachlan Macquarie. They were strategically positioned on the main routes between Sydney, Parramatta, the Hawkesbury and, later, Goulburn and the Blue Mountains. It was Macquarie who instigated the reforms and directions that give us today's variety of drinking houses.

Which is the oldest pub in the nation?

There are several claimants to the title of oldest pub, and the answer is not cut and dried. A hotel might be operating under an original licence, but may have moved location or changed its name. Or a hotel's licence may have been suspended, either at the discretion of the publican or the licensing authorities. Below are listed the genuine claimants to the title, apart from the aforementioned Woolpack Inn.

Hobart's Hope and Anchor Tavern was licensed as the Hope Inn to Francis Barnes in 1818, then was known as the Hope and Anchor in 1823, and the Alexandra Hotel in 1901. Recently the proprietors of the two-storey waterfront pub have claimed that, as it stands on the site of the Whale Fishery Hotel (licensed in 1807), it is the country's oldest hotel still on its original site. This may never be confirmed, as the records kept by officials in early Hobart are not complete.

Also in Tasmania, the Bush Inn at New Norfolk was built in 1815 by Ann Bridger. It was not licensed until ten years after, but has been licensed ever since, in its original location and under its original name. Even though the structure of the Bush Inn is older than the Hope and Anchor, it was not licensed until 1825, seven years later than the first official records of the Hobart pub.

The Surveyor-General Inn at Berrima in New South Wales' Southern Highlands was licensed on 29 June 1835 to William Harper, who had named his hotel in honour of his immediate superior, Major Thomas Mitchell. In 1961, the licensing court threatened to demolish this hotel which claims to be the country's oldest continuously licensed pub. Fortunately the small community's other hotels and businesses rallied to save the Surveyor-General pub, and it now operates under the new 'Historic Inn' licence, which circumvents the usual licensing and building laws.

Further north at Windsor is the Macquarie Arms. Built in 1815 on land granted to emancipated convict Richard Fitzgerald on condition that he build a two-storey hotel. It was opened on 26 July of the same year by Governor Macquarie, who had given Fitzgerald those instructions. For five years between 1835 and 1840 the hotel was used as the officers' mess of the 50th Regiment, and later from 1840 until 1870 it was an unlicensed private residence.

Two favourite contenders in The Rocks, Sydney, can be discounted. Even though the Lord Nelson Hotel (built 1834) is the oldest hotel in Sydney, it is quite some way from being the oldest pub in the country. Nearby, the much loved and photographed wedge-shaped Hero of Waterloo is younger than the Lord Nelson by at least nine years.

For the record, the oldest hotels in states and territories besides Tasmania and New South Wales are: Port Albert Hotel in Port Albert, Victoria (1842); the Farmers Arms at Cabarlah in Queensland's Darling Downs (1862); the Victoria Hotel in Darwin, which opened as the North Australian in 1882; the Stirling Arms at Guildford in suburban Perth (1850s); the Edinburgh Castle Hotel, which opened in Adelaide's city centre in 1837 and has traded under that name ever since; and the Canberra Hotel, at Yarralumla, which started trading after the repeal of prohibitionist laws in 1928. Refurbished, it is now the Hyatt Hotel Canberra.

To boutique and back

The trend for tavern-style hotels where accommodation is eschewed in favour of food and drink, can be traced to the late 1970s. So-called 'taverns' boomed in the central business districts of most cities for nearly ten years, but in the main they were part of a shallow marketing push designed to capture drinkers and not much else.

During the 1980s there was a move to improve hotel dining-rooms, with some pubs incorporating restaurants into their establishments.

The next logical progression was the boutique brewery, where hotels either brewed their own beer or exclusively sold beer brewed by specialist brewers like Hahn and Scharer and Kent Town. Hahn was later to become well-known to mainstream beer drinkers after its takeover by the Lion Nathan conglomerate.

Western Australia led the way into the boutique market at the Sail and Anchor Tavern in Fremantle. Originally the Freemason's, it was built in 1903 as a two-storey hotel, and was converted in 1983 into the country's first micro-brewery by the Brewtech group, changing its name at the same time.

Hotels such as the Imperial in the Sunshine Coast town of Eumundi, the Waterloo in Brisbane, St Ives in Hobart's suburban Sandy Bay, the Loaded Dog in Melbourne's Fitzroy, the Lord Nelson in Sydney, the Old Lion in North Adelaide, Port Dock Brewery in Port Adelaide and the Earl of Aberdeen in Adelaide introduced punters to the new, and initially successful, boutique breweries.

Bendigo's Rifle Brigade Hotel has proved that you don't have to be in the city to grab a slice of the boutique beer market, as have the George IV Inn at Picton NSW, Geelong's Scottish Chiefs Hotel, and the Dinner Plains Village in Victoria's snow country.

Old Lion, North Adelaide, SA

Some firsts

In South Australia's Riverland, as well as on the West Coast and in Western Australia, you will find various examples of the 'community hotel'. In the proposals for these hotels – to be run using the 'Gothenburg' system – the townsfolk would own the hotel, provide quality accommodation, food and drink, and then share in the profits. When the Renmark Community Hotel opened in 1897, it was the first of its kind in the British Empire, and one of the first in the world. In later years, some of the proceeds went towards the maintenance of parks and gardens, the district hospital, show society, welfare agencies and sporting clubs. Berri and Barmera have first-class examples of community hotels, as do some West Coast towns including Ceduna and Streaky Bay.

The *Sydney Morning Herald* was first printed from John Redman's Keep Within Compass Hotel in George Street in 1831. And the country's first regular postal service operated from Isaac Nichols' Sydney Hotel in 1809.

The first (illegal) meeting of the Freemasons was held at the St Patrick Hotel on Sydney's George Street on 16 May 1803.

The first hotel to have a private bar was the former Liverpool Arms Hotel in 1850. Edward Samuel changed the name of his Sydney hotel from the Black Boy, and in doing so set apart the nation's first private bar, offering a peaceful venue for merchants and others to talk business.

On 2 January 1838 John Burke left from the former Lamb Inn, Melbourne (later to be known as Scott's) on his epic journey to Yass, NSW, as part of the first overland mail service to Sydney. When the hotel met with a spectacular end on Christmas Eve 1839 it became the first pub in Australia to be demolished by a keg of gunpowder!

The first trunk call made in the nation was from the Bush Inn in New Norfolk, Tasmania, by proprietor Captain Blockley in 1888.

The former College Arms Hotel in Adelaide was Australia's first commercial training hotel. The building had served as a hotel since 1846 under a multitude of different names. It was jointly operated by the Australian Hotels Association, the Liquor Trades Union of SA, and the Department of TAFE (School of Tourism and Hospitality), and was redeveloped at a cost of $1.2 million.

The Elephant's Foot Hotel in Paddington was Sydney's first totally non-smoking hotel. It was opened by manager Steve Horell on Thursday 1 April 1993, following on from the smoke-free bars at the Unicorn Hotel in Paddington.

The first drive-in bottle shop in the world opened at Highway Inn, Plympton, in suburban Adelaide on 1 October 1955. The idea belonged to local businessman Clive Dundas.

Striking out

The former Albert Hotel in Castlemaine, Victoria, hosted a farewell for explorers Robert O'Hara Burke (who was the town's constable) and William Wills before their epic journey to the Gulf of Carpentaria. They also stayed at the Maiden's in Menindee, NSW, on their way north.

Explorer Edward John Eyre spent some time at the former Sherrat's Family Hotel in Albany, Western Australia, in 1840 and on his overland venture from Adelaide in July 1841.

John and Alexander Forrest departed from the Geraldton Hotel in Western Australia on their second crossing of the continent from west to east in 1874. The party reached the Peake Overland Telegraph Station in South Australia after seven months, by then they were suffering from thirst. Forrest has a hotel named after him in the Western Australian port town of Bunbury.

A warm reception greeted Norwegian antarctic pioneer Raold Amundsen when he stayed at Hadley's Orient Hotel in Hobart after becoming the first man to reach the South Pole in 1912.

Medical moments

The bodies of Thomas Coulsen, licensee of the former New Inn in Cessnock, New South Wales, and his brother John were found in the Freemason's Hotel in Sydney in 1840, the cause of death being 'delirium tremens'.

At the Criterion Hotel in Rockhampton, Queensland in 1900, a waiter at the nearby Sydney Hotel was found to be ill with the Plague. Twenty-eight guests at the Criterion, including two members of the Legislative Council, were quarantined at the hotel. In 1919 the Prince of Wales Hotel at Nowra was quarantined, this time during the pneumonic influenza pandemic of 1919. The publican's wife, Alice Parkes, succumbed to the disease.

A bizarre incident occurred in 1905 at the former Bokhara Inn, 25 miles north-west of Brewarrina, NSW, when a drunken crowd decided to open the head of an even drunker companion, 'to see how he worked'. The cause of death was deemed to be brain damage.

Patients from the Heidelberg Repatriation Hospital imbibed at the nearby Ivanhoe Hotel, nicknaming the publican 'Doc' Ryan.

In the spring of 1919, the local board of health took over both the Mount Barker and the Park Hotels in Western Australia during an outbreak of influenza. But another medical condition, dyslexia, afflicted these two pubs later. The Park Hotel at the northern end of town is known as the 'bottom' pub, and is the home of players from the South Mount Barker Football Club. Conversely the Mount Barker at the southern side is known as the 'top' hotel and is the favourite of players from the North Mount Barker Football Club.

When property developer Mark Foy bought the Belgravia Hotel at the turn of the century he turned the complex into a 'hydropathic establishment'. The health-spa was not very successful in that location, but in later years it became a popular mountain retreat. Another 'spa' resort was at the Hot Springs Hotel in Innot Hot Springs, far northern Queensland.

Practical joking

In the Jolly Swagman Hotel in Mungindi, NSW, a prankster once attached the metal strip that surrounded the edge of the bar to a battery. It was the source of great mirth whenever a newcomer rested his elbows on the metal bar. The prankster went on to become a respected member of the Queensland police.

Publican James Thompson was riding into Mungindi with a new chum Englishman and a friendly conversation started. The Englishman suggested a race to the pub, with the loser having to buy the other a beer. Thompson thought about this, then upped the bet to include the whole bar. The race started, with the Englishman, who received a head start from Thompson, seemingly ahead by miles. He arrived at the bar, cursing folk who couldn't see a bet through, only to find Thompson at the crowded bar, waiting for his drink. Thompson had taken a short-cut, and rounded up all the townsfolk he knew for a beer on the new chum.

Jim Blore, mine host of the Family in Tibooburra, NSW, in the early 1950s, was cleaning out his loo – which in those days meant burning off the excess paper using a quantity of diesel poured down one of the holes of the two-hole toilet. Jim forgot the matches, and in the time it took to him get some from inside the hotel, the postmaster sat down on the second toilet. Coming back and tossing a match in the first hole, Jim heard the flames rush out and then an anguished yelp, followed by the postie emerging from the number two dunny with his trousers around his ankles. The postie vowed that from that day onwards he would only use the number one seat.

A duel is said to have been fought at the Union Hotel in Devonport, Tasmania, between Adye Douglas and Captain R.H. Davies. A gaggle of practical jokers placed a blank in Davies pistol, and in Douglas's they inserted a package of raspberry jam. On firing, Davies was alarmed to put his hands to his forehead to find a red mass that he thought were his brains. The onlookers fell about, but Davies was not amused.

2

'Tell 'em I died game'

One reason bushrangers are often linked to pubs is that it was too easy and too tempting for them to combine business with pleasure. Travel through western New South Wales, Victoria and even western Queensland for any fair distance and you will come across a publican claiming some sort of 'bushranger' heritage for his establishment. Although some will be telling the truth, the majority have probably used their imaginations. But if you are visiting the Highlands area pubs in Victoria, and you come across a plaque stating that Ned Kelly or his gang drank here, take heed – the reign of that renegade was inextricably linked with the hotels, inns and shanties of the district.

Such . . . is life

Early in his life Ned Kelly, his brother Dan, Steve Hart, Joe Byrne and some others formed a loose gang known as the 'Greta Mob'. They were recognisable from the way they wore their hats' chin-straps under their noses. It was in the pubs of Greta and Benalla and other towns that the Kellys started their careers in petty crime – mostly selling stolen horses. This often led to brawls with the colonial policemen, for instance in Benalla on 17 September 1879, when a drunken Ned was arrested after riding his horse along the footpath.

He maintained that the publican had drugged him, but the seed was sown for Kelly's hatred of the Victorian police.

The very next day Kelly met Violet Town policeman Thomas Lonigan for the first time and, after a heated exchange about the previous days' incident, Ned uttered the prophetic words: 'I've never shot a man yet, Lonigan, but if I ever do, so help me God, you'll be the first!' Fourteen months later Kelly was tried and hanged for Lonigan's murder.

It appears that Benalla was the Kelly gang's real stomping-ground, often drowning the dust in one of the town's 17 hotels. One barman remembered that 'Ned Kelly was of a cordial disposition, but Dan Kelly was inclined to be sullen or morose . . . At times they would gallop up and down the streets shouting and singing, for which they were fined several times'.

Many hotels in the north-east and Highlands districts of Victoria also claim Kelly heritage. Tanswell's Commercial Hotel in Beechworth is one, the Plough Inn at Tarrawingee another. A stolen horse accompanied Ned to Wangaratta's now defunct Star Hotel, and in Beechworth, at the Imperial Hotel in 1874, Ned fought and beat long time acquaintance 'Wild' Wright for what was called the 'Unofficial Heavyweight boxing crown of north-eastern Victoria'.

On the weekend of 8–10 February 1879 Ned Kelly and his gang rode into the town of Jerilderie and carried out one of the best planned and most successful of their raids. Beforehand, they had duped a riverside publican into lending them his boat to transport them across the Murray River into New South Wales, then gauged the town's opinions of the Kelly Gang while hiding at Robinson's Woolpack Inn. What Ned and his crew found out surprised even them. It appeared that the good people of Jerilderie did not fear the gang, but in fact revered them for their courage! Armed with this knowledge, Dan Kelly and Joe Byrne bailed up the local troopers, donned their uniforms and proceeded to round up the locals and hold them hostage in Cox's Royal Mail Hotel.

Apparently the perfect kidnappers (and good Catholic boys to boot) the gang helped the constable's wife prepare the Court House for Sunday Mass, but the next day Ned and Steve Hart relieved the Bank of New South Wales of well over £2000.

On their way back to the Royal Mail Hotel, Kelly and Hart, with the bank manager in tow, stopped off at McDougall's Albion Hotel, where it is said that Ned shouted the whole bar, although not partaking of any liquor himself. It was at the Royal Mail that Ned Kelly drafted his famous 'Jerilderie Letter'. Now classified by the National Trust, the Royal Mail Hotel commemorates its heritage in the shape of the Kelly Bar, complete with a Kelly in armour at the front door.

When the Kelly Gang struck, pubs were often the cornerstone of their plans. Steve Hart and Joe Byrne checked out the country town Euroa from the impressive North Eastern Hotel before one hold-up. Hart met the town's only policeman outside the pub – he failed to recognise the outlaw!

The 'last stand' of the Kelly gang has been well documented, but historians are still confused as to why the four bushrangers chose to have the inevitable confrontation at Ann Jones' Glenrowan Inn, rather than McDonald's (or M'Donnell's) Railway Tavern, south of the railway line, which they frequented often. By then much of the north-east of Victoria was clearly polarised, and the publican at the Railway was a Kelly sympathiser whereas Jones was not. The gang rendezvoused at

McDonald's, and put their horses up there, but gathered 62 townsfolk of Glenrowan and kept them hostage at the Glenrowan Inn.

The outlaws were awaiting the results of a trap they had set, in which a train carrying troops from Wangaratta was to be derailed. It all went horribly wrong for them when a captive duped the gang into releasing him, and ran to the train line just in time to warn the driver. The train stopped without damage, and troops soon gathered outside the Glenrowan Inn.

A lengthy battle followed, leaving a couple of hostages (including Jones' baby son) as well as Hart, Byrne and Dan Kelly dead. Ned confronted the troops in his suit of armour and was caught, tried for murder, and sentenced to hang in Melbourne Gaol. It is said that even when Ned was hanged, it was at 'Castieau's Hotel', the slang name for Melbourne Gaol, after the gaol's Governor, J.B.Castieau.

So who said that pubs don't bring out the best in people!

The Glenrowan Inn no longer stands. It was razed by the troops whilst flushing out the gang, although the bar from the Railway Tavern still exists at the Glenrowan Tourist Centre, restored by proprietor Don Tibbits and his wife Valda. They have recreated the 'last stand' using a fibreglass cast of a cottage that looked similar to Ann Jones' hotel.

Bushrangers had a love of colourful names. Captain Starlight stuck up the Enngonia Hotel, NSW and at the same time shot a policeman, while the Wonbobbie Inn near Warren, NSW, was treated to a visit by Midnight. Unfortunately Midnight showed no courtesy to his host by shooting his wife stone dead.

Such is . . . death!

Pubs have often been the last resting places of outlaws. Harry Law met his maker at the Enngonia Hotel in north-western NSW; Jimmy Governor was laid out at the Caledonian Hotel in Singleton, NSW for a coronial hearing: and so-called 'gentleman bushranger' Jacky Jacky (William Westwood) was captured at the Lake George Hotel at Bungendore, NSW, and banished to Norfolk Island where he was hanged, aged 26. In 1867, a bushranger named Rutherford was mortally wounded at the Pine Ridge Hotel at Eenaweena, near Warren, NSW, when he came off second best after a struggle with publican Beauvais. The Country Club Hotel at Yea, Victoria was not only a bar, but also a makeshift morgue that once held a bushranger named Cosgrove who was shot by the troopers in the town.

Innocent bystanders were more often the victims of bushrangers. John Kennedy Hume, brother of explorer Hamilton Hume and an explorer himself, was shot dead by bushrangers at the Telegraph Hotel in Gunning, NSW, in 1840.

Policemen often had promising careers cut short by lawless robbers as well. One was killed at Hobart's Blue Bells of Scotland Inn by Martin Cash, another at Nerrigundah on the NSW South Coast when the Golden Fleece Hotel was held up by bushrangers, and Constable Miles O'Grady was fatally wounded on 9 April 1866 after he killed Fletcher, the leader of a bushranging gang.

At the Bushranger Hotel at Collector, NSW, Ben Hall's sidekick, John Dunn, shot and killed Constable Samuel Nelson on 26 January 1865. Nelson was after Hall, Dunn and Johnny Gilbert. A memorial at the hotel celebrates his bravery.

There was a sly grog house, the Robert Burns Inn at Castlemaine, Victoria, where notorious bushranger 'Mad Dog' Morgan drank when he was just plain Danny Morgan, butcher.

The lads from the Lachlan

Whatever the good people of Canowindra, NSW were expecting on the morning of 12 October 1863, it probably wasn't incarceration at one of the town's few pubs. On that morning bushrangers Ben Hall, John Gilbert, John O'Meally, Michael Burke and John Vane rode in from Carcoar, bailed up the town's lone constable, and ushered him, along with the other forty locals, into the Miner's Arms Hotel. Here the townsfolk were searched for hidden arms, and their horses were rounded-up and yarded within sight of the hotel as a precaution against escape.

An extraordinary three-day party followed – attendance was compulsory. Hall and his gang supplied food, drinks and smokes courtesy of the hotel's till. A Miss O'Flanagan provided the music, and some of the outlaws 'entertained' their unfortunate guests with demonstrations of their proficiency with firearms. The five bushrangers drank very little, but they impressed their prisoners with their self-confidence, even confiding details of their hold-ups. Hall made little effort to rob his captors, preferring to use the exercise as an example of the power he and his men could enforce. When the money had run out, the outlaws bad farewell to their hostages and sped off on horseback, blazing their revolvers over their heads in exhilaration.

Tragedy struck twelve days later with the gunning down of teenager Micky Burke. John Vane went straight, but was eventually put to trial and sentenced to 15 years.

O'Meally was shot during a hold-up attempt, and Hall and Gilbert were joined by young tearaway Johnny Dunn. The trio continued on their way until dobbed in by Dunn's grandfather, John Kelly. Acting on his information troopers ambushed the gang and Ben Hall was killed on 5 May 1865. Gilbert was killed in a shoot-out eight later, while Dunn went to trial after he was captured in the gun-battle. He was hanged.

 At Seymour a certain 'Whiteheaded Bob' kept authorities at bay at the original Seymour Hotel for some days in the late 1840s.

A bolt from the blue

Captain Thunderbolt is one name that comes up regularly in hotels in the north of New South Wales. In one productive month – December 1865 – Thunderbolt held up the Squatters Arms (Collarenebri), Cook's (Quirindi) and Davis's (Currabubula). He ran into bad luck at Griffin's (Carroll), where he had a shoot-out with police, and at the Meroe Inn he was outsmarted during a hold-up.

The publican, Henry Chambers, saved the cash kept at the hotel by tossing it through an open window into a woodpile when he heard Thunderbolt and his side-kick approaching. It is also said that Chambers saved a patron's expensive watch. The watch's ticking was so loud that Chambers thought Thunderbolt would be on it like a flash, so he picked up an accordion and began to play loudly. When told to raise his arms above his head, Chambers kept up the music, and

Thunderbolt polka'd away with only a fraction of the available booty.

Never a shy bushranger, Captain Thunderbolt once took the opportunity to enjoy the opening night festivities at the Red Lion Hotel in Dalby in one of his sojourns over the northern border.

Tasmanian bushranger, Tom Rares, was kept hidden at Hobart's Man At The Wheel Hotel following his daring escape from the Port Arthur Penal Colony.

Robin Hood

Across Bass Strait a bushranger named Martin Cash was known as the 'Robin Hood of Van Diemens Land' because he was rarely violent. In 1843, however, he was driven to violence at the Woolpack Inn at Gretna during a vicious battle with police. Soon after he shot and killed a policeman at Hobart's Bluebells of Scotland Inn and was sentenced to life on Norfolk Island, later commuted to ten years. On his return to Tasmania, Cash lived a quiet life, growing apples at his farm at Glenorchy, and was one of very few bushrangers to die of old age.

While actors were filming the Glenrowan Inn scenes in a cottage at Mitcham, Melbourne, for Australia's first-ever feature film, *The Story of the Kelly Gang*, the fake brawl turned real. For authenticity's sake the Melbourne dead-beats hired as extras were given real beer, and as the day became hotter so did the tempers. Police were called in to end the fighting.

Pub fraternity

On 15 September 1892 during a damaging and controversial strike, 30 police with fixed bayonets charged into the Theatre Royal Hotel in Broken Hill, which was hosting a meeting of the Labour Defence Committee, and arrested the leaders.

In 1909 Broken Hill strike leader Tom Mann was effectively banned from speaking in New South Wales following his arrest after taking part in a protest march. So the Cockburn Hotel just across the South Australian border became a most unlikely venue for a union meeting. A convoy of forty trucks and half a dozen carriages carrying Mann's supporters left Broken Hill on 31 January 1909 for Cockburn. A similar journey occurred on 12 April that same year, to hear Mann championing the socialist cause and denouncing capitalists. The strike lasted from January to May.

In October 1931 Carlton and United Breweries ceased to deliver beer to the Hotel Australia in Melbourne at the request of the Victorian Licensed Victuallers Association after the manager of the hotel, Mr N.D. Carlyon, stimulated trade by offering a free counter lunch at the hotel's bar. The management was unrepentant and said that they would continue the practice, believing it to be a legitimate way of stimulating business.

The ultimate sacrifice was made in Horsham in Victoria, Mulline in WA, and Darwin when drinkers went on strike! In these towns the pubs had colluded to fix a high price on beer. Drinkers refused to drink at the pubs and instead organised bottled supplies from nearby towns. In Darwin the customer boycott was the result of a government monopoly on hotels that produced poor standards of service, value and hygiene.

The Ship, Dock & General Labourers Union was formed at the Royal Oak Hotel, Balmain, in 1887. It gradually evolved into the Painters & Dockers Federation, merging into today's Maritime Union of Australia. Near the Royal Oak, the Exchange Hotel was the early venue for meetings of the Balmain Labourers Union, another predecessor of the MUA.

When called the Bristol Tavern, the Franklin Hotel in Adelaide was the meeting place of the Trades and Labour Council from its creation in 1884 to 1888 when the first Trades Hall was built. In the northern city of Port Pirie, the International Hotel in the the 1880s was the venue for meetings of the Working Men's Association, the forerunner to the Waterside Workers Union.

As the Belvidere Hotel, the Eastern Hill Hotel in Fitzroy became the head-quarters of the Stonemason's Union (later merged with the Carpenter's Union). It was here that local MLA Dr Thomas Embling came up with the slogan 'Eight Hours labour, Eight Hours recreation, Eight Hours rest'.

The Imperial Hotel at Clifton on the south coast of New South Wales was declared 'black' by unionists in 1938 when the publican supposedly insulted ladies collecting for a strike fund. Trade dropped by 50 per cent and the publican cut his losses and decided to leave the hotel business.

Controversy raged at the Esplanade Hotel in Perth when a disruptive strike was led by maverick union legend Cecilia Shelley in March 1921. The main grievances were the conditions offered for women in the bar and cleaning areas, and the employment of Asian immigrants for cheap wages.

3

Feeding time at the zoo

Not all the colourful characters in our pubs have been human. A couple of regulars at the Silverton Hotel in outback New South Wales are Mr Mac, a beer swilling cockatoo, and Jake, a three-legged foxy cross who sports a 'Do Not Feed' sign in green fluorescent paint across his white back. Publicans Colin and Ines McLeod fear that passers-by will feel sorry for Jake and feed him so many treats that his three legs will not be able to carry his weight anymore.

At the Silverton Hotel years before, publican John Stokie received a bad batch of beer from Terowie, South Australia. He put it out in the open, believing that the fresh air might render it suitable for drinking. Leaving an old-timer in charge to keep the curious goats at bay, Stokie was later alarmed to discover both the old man and the goats passed out after drinking the contents.

Dogs are by far the most common pub pets. The Swan Hotel in Richmond, Victoria was said to have been frequented by an alcoholic dog, Nigger, who had his own mug and bar stool. If he found anyone on his stool he would walk out; if they were still there when he came back he would bite them. If Richmond football club won, the dog would get so drunk he would have to be carried home. A local policeman used to take the dog on his night rounds and Nigger would be offered bones and biscuits. He also made a regular visit to the abattoir on Sundays for beer and liver.

In the Tibooburra floods of March 1949, aircraft were used to drop off supplies to some of the remote stations. At one of them the aircraft crews met with 'Tubby' Martin's dog, Digger. Martin was the publican of the 'Two Storey' (as the Royal Hotel was nicknamed), and Digger was renowned for drinks cadging. No one could resist giving the mutt a beer, and after a few he became relaxed and sedate, if a little unsteady on his legs. Later, the old cat would come in to a warm welcome from Digger. The next day Digger would revert to his old self, chasing and scaring the wits out of the cat. They said that Digger just couldn't stand cats when he had a hangover.

Fishy tales and lizard lounges

The most famous patron of the former Wyalong Hotel in NSW was Jack Clancy, who would empty his bag of snakes (and consequently, the bar) if he did not receive a free drink. The Wyalong Hotel was delicensed in the 1930s, and dismantled and moved to Kikiora, eighty-seven kilometres away. It is not known if Clancy was invited to the re-opening.

An unusual incident occurred at the Imperial Hotel in Clifton, NSW, in 1913, when a stranger brought a snake into the bar and an argument followed about whether the snake was venomous. To prove his point a doubter placed his finger in the snake's mouth. A coronial inquest found later that William Aubrey Grieveson died from snakebite, and the man who brought the snake into the bar was 'deserving of severe censure'.

Further along the coast, visitors to the South Gippsland town of

Wonthaggi are stunned by the entrance to Taberner's Whalebone Hotel. Jack (Cobber) Keighley, butcher, and Harold Playdell, miner, were unemployed in 1923 when a 74-foot whale was washed up at Wonthaggi Beach. They boiled down the whale in coppers on the beach, and netted £40 for their effort. The jawbones were sold to Charles Taberner for £25. In 1974 the Borough Council was forced to amend its bylaws to allow Taberner's Hotel to be the only building in the town to retain its verandah posts, and therefore its whalebones.

There couldn't be too many hotels that have a sea creature as concierge. Francis Bauer, the first licensee of the Isle of Wight Hotel at Cowes on Phillip Island, kept a pet seal called Jack who performed that duty (as best he could).

Some avant-garde architecture is on display at the Gagudju Hotel in Kakadu National Park – it has been built in the shape of a giant crocodile. The entrance to the two-storey complex is through the jaws of the croc, with the heart simulated by the central swimming pools. Built at a cost of $13 million, it was designed by John Wilkins, who was also the architect of Darwin's rebuilt Christchurch Cathedral.

Another reptilian institution is the Birdsville Hotel in Queensland, perhaps the most famous pub in the country. The hotel becomes the focal point of the outback on the first weekend in September when the annual Birdsville Cup horse-race is run. The Birdsville Hotel is also known as the international club-rooms of the Green Lizard League, formed during a beer shortage in 1968, when all the patrons had to drink was Creme-de-Menthe.

Until 1930 the kitchen of The Portland Bay Hotel, Victoria, was paved with the crushed vertebra of whales caught in the bay.

Tiger tales

Tasmanian hunters must have enjoyed the sport on offer in the hinterland of the state's wild west coast, as early advertisements for the Whale's Head Hotel at Mount Balfour show the hotel offered tiger shooting, among other pleasantries. The 'tigers' were probably Tasmanian Tigers, now believed to be extinct. The hotel become extinct sometime in the early 1930s.

Shooter Tom Donovan brought the carcass of the legendary 'Tantanoola Tiger' into the bar of the Railway Hotel at Tantanoola in South Australia in 1895. The district had supposedly been so 'terrorised' by the animal that a large hunt was undertaken. Mystery surrounded the beast, but it turned out to be a type of Assyrian wolf that probably escaped during a shipwrecking on the rugged south-east coast. The stuffed animal is displayed at the pub, along with Donovan's rifle. Famous Adelaide wordsmith, Max Harris, wrote a poem about the beast and the hotel, which became known as the Tiger Hotel in the 1930s.

The hotel in the Northern Territory truckstop town of Dunmarra was showered by fish in mid-February 1994. Meteorologists had trouble explaining the phenomenon, especially given that the hotel is 600 miles inland.

Horsing around

At the Richmond Arms in Tasmania, Basset Dickson attempted to
ride his horse up the stairs. It got half-way up, froze, and would not
budge. It took several men to rectify the situation.

An incident that would have embarrassed Harold V. Piesse of the
Katanning Hotel in Western Australia for a long time was the time he
rode a horse to the top balcony of this hotel in 1904 and a block-and-
tackle was needed to bring it back to terra firma.

In 1923 at West Wyalong, NSW, a horse had a lucky escape when
it fell into the Commercial Hotel's underground tank. The 27,000
litres of water were pumped out by the Fire Brigade, and the horse
was finally rescued, again with the help of a block-and-tackle.

Horses people can cope with, but a lady visitor to the
Transcontinental Hotel in Oodnadatta was alarmed to find a stray
camel in the passage, and startled when it started to chase her.
Drinkers in the hotel eventually coaxed the animal out of the pub
using pool cues, but no amount of encouragement could get the lady
to prolong her stay.

The Bald Faced Stag Hotel in Leichhardt, NSW, was named after a
deer frequently seen in the Five Dock district. The hotel was a part of
the lives of the Hearn family from 1830 until it was sold to Tooheys in
1970. The link between the deer and the hotel goes back to when one
of the founders of the brewery, John Thomas Toohey, produced a
beer that he named Stag, after the hotel. A stag also featured in the
brewer's logo.

Richmond Arms Hotel, Richmond, Tasmania

Elephant's trunk

The Sir Joseph Banks Hotel at Botany, NSW, was the first venue in the country to contain zoological and botanical gardens, opened not long after the hotel. Elephants, Bengal tigers and bears were among the animals exhibited.

Charles Matthews, licensee of the Gepps Cross Hotel in South Australia, had a pet elephant he had bought from the Unley Zoo (part of the old Cremorne Hotel Gardens). The first elephant in the state, it was put to good use pulling out bogged vehicles and was involved in the heavy lifting of the railway from Islington to Salisbury. In ploughing matches the elephant would win a lot of money for his owner, who in turn rewarded his friend with the odd bucket of beer.

Polly wanna cracker? Nah, make it a pint

The pet bird in the beer garden at the Adelaide River Hotel, Northern
Territory, should have considered itself fortunate to live a long life.
The parrot would swear constantly at the clientele, and could make
noises as deafening as a dog-fight. The bird's owner was once offered
£150 for it, but refused. Cocky died first, the owner soon followed,
and now bird and owner occupy the same grave.

Another famous bird was Alec Mudie's crow, who lived with his
owner at the Federal Hotel at Bemboka in southern NSW. The bird
drank the dregs from the glasses at the bar, then struggled to walk a
straight line drawn in chalk by Mudie. The crow could also talk –
one of its best lines: 'Put me to bed, Alec, I'm as drunk as an owl.'
(Or so they say.)

Once a boarder set to work teaching Mudie's crow to swear using
a visiting politician's name. The said pollie grew flustered when,
during his speech, he couldn't work out where the heckling was coming
from. As soon as he cottoned on, the politician made an offer to
Mudie for the crow, which was refused. When Alec Mudie died
his crow stopped talking, could never again be persuaded to utter a
single word.

Mrs Hardy, the wife of the publican of the Four Posts Hotel at
Jarklin, Victoria, had an invalid son who owned a cockatoo that would
fly along with the car whenever his owner was taken for a drive.
When the boy died, the cocky would make a daily flight from the hotel
to the cemetery to pay his respects. The cocky was once stolen from
the pub and sold to a hotel in Kerang, which promptly returned it
when the bird piped up with 'I'm Hardy's cockatoo'! Known mainly
for eating 'Tick Tock' biscuits and for picking fights with customers,

he again fell foul of kidnappers in late 1990 – by then he was sixty-five. He has never been returned.

The Eagle on the Hill Hotel in the Adelaide Hills was first named the Eagle's Nest around 1859, after the large wedge-tailed eagle kept in a cage on the front verandah. When the hotel burnt down in 1899 and was rebuilt, the live eagle was replaced with a carved one. Destroyed again in the Ash Wednesday fires of 1983, the hotel was rebuilt as a tavern, but kept the eagle statue.

Cane toad races are held at Queensland's Airlie Beach Hotel in the Garden Lounge each Tuesday and Thursday evening, and at Balmain's Dry Dock, Port Adelaide's Royal Arms, and Collingwood's Baden Powell Hotel punters are treated to hermit crab races. At the Baden Powell bets are laid on the first crustacean home, the losers donating a percentage of their wagers to charity.

Beer gardens

A tree was planted at the front of the Oatley Hotel in southern Sydney in memory of John O'Grady, a man who contributed much to pub culture. Through his classic *They're a Weird Mob* (written under the alias Nino Culotta) and many other books, O'Grady helped to demystify colloquial Australian language with great humour and insight.

The former Old Grapevine Hotel, built in 1866 at Chiltern, Victoria, replaced the original Star Hotel. In the courtyard is a grapevine the same age as the hotel. The vine has a 155 centimetre circumference, and is said to be one of the largest grape vines in the world.

Willows near the Trawool Valley Resort Hotel in north-eastern Victoria are said to have come from cuttings from the willow on Napoleon Bonaparte's St Helena gravesite.

A famous tree grew in front of the former Terminus Hotel in Darwin. It was so well-known that it became the mailing address for some townsfolk. A gathering place and public forum, the tree gained notoriety when chief medical officer Dr Mervyn Holmes, who was considering condemning the pub, claimed it was the best part of the hotel. The tree was one of few landmarks that survived Japanese air-raids, and still stands today in Cavanagh Street. It is known to locals as the 'Tree of Knowledge'.

Another famous Tree of Knowledge grows across the road from the Railway Hotel in Barcaldine, Queensland. It was the meeting-place for shearers involved in the 1891 strike during which it is said that the foundations of the Australian Labor Party were laid.

Opening in July 1989, the Tall Trees Hotel at Smithton, Tasmania, was built using native timber such as Huon Pine, Native Olive, Goldywood, Native Plum, Leatherwood, Myrtle, Sassafras, Celery Top Pine and Blackwood. As it was mostly made from timber, it took only nineteen weeks to build.

Aquatic adventures

Some bad planning spelled the end for the Miena Hotel in central Tasmania. It was ear-marked for demolition when the Hydro Electric Authority wanted extra capacity for the lake nearby, which meant raising the dam wall and flooding the countryside, including the old pub. The hotel was demolished, but when the works were completed the site was left standing high and dry.

At least three other pubs have been inundated by a reservoir. The owners of the Millbrook Hotel in the Adelaide Hills forfeited their licence for £1600 compensation during the construction of the Kangaroo Creek Dam in 1914, the nearby Morning Star Hotel in Chain of Ponds went under in 1978, and the original Advancetown Hotel on the Gold Coast was rebuilt on higher ground after the creation of the Hinze Dam.

The Commercial Hotel in Clermont, Queensland, was relocated after flooding of Sandy Creek and The Lagoon in 1916. The L-shaped building was moved in two pieces from its original location in Drummond Street across The Lagoon, over the high-water mark and into Capella Street.

The Grand View Hotel in Cleveland, Queensland, opened in 1849 when the locality was touted as a port. Two disastrous shipwrecks followed, and the area became known as Bigge's Folly, Bigge being the builder of the hotel.

During construction of part of the Caledonian Inn in Robe, South Australia, ships' doors and some of the timbers used came from the Dutch ship *Koning Willem de Tweede* and the *Phaeton*, both of which were wrecked in Guichen Bay.

In Robe's early days the South Australian coastal town had no hall, and functions were held in a big room at the Caledonian Inn. In 1861 the ships *Alma* and *Livingstone* were in port to pick up shipments of wool, and a ball was held to entertain the crews from the ships. Neither of the ships ever left the port. One of the fiercest storms ever known in the area drove them ashore, and barring some wool salvaged from the *Livingstone*, both ships were a total loss.

4

Pressing the flesh

Politicians of all persuasions have always liked to be seen among the 'common people' and during election campaigns most fail to resist the temptation of being photographed in a pub. While the stereotype of Liberal party politicians preferring the sanctity and opulence of clubs, and Labor members enjoying the comradeship of the local pub may ring true, from time to time these lines are blurred.

Labor pains

In 1891 pastoralists in Queensland insisted on using non-union labour in their shearing sheds, angering shearers camped outside the town of Barcaldine waiting for work. It was usual for the shearers to camp together while awaiting employment, but this time it was a lengthy stay. About 1000 shearers armed themselves, hoisted the Southern Cross and in a show of solidarity sang Henry Lawson's 'Freedom on the Wallaby'. The men met under the Tree of Knowledge in front of the Railway Hotel in Barcaldine, then marched along the main street.

After three months the strike was broken by constables and soldiers brought into the district and the leaders were arrested and given sentences of three years with hard labour. The Pastoralists Association also won the right to bring in non-union labour to shear their sheep, which fuelled the formation of the Australian Labor Party. A member of the strike committee, Thomas Joseph Ryan, became leader of the Queensland ALP in 1912, and the party's first premier in 1915.

A meeting of the Northcote Workingman's Democratic Association was held in 1891 at the Commercial Hotel in Northcote, Victoria. This organisation was one of the founding branches of the Trades Hall Progressive Political League, which was a forerunner to the ALP. The building was condemned as unsafe by the Northcote Council in 1894 and sold for removal for £3000.

The Colac Hotel in Port Adelaide is the unofficial headquarters of the Australian Labor Party in that traditional Labor-oriented area. The Breakfast Creek Hotel in suburban Albion fulfils the same role in Brisbane.

Strange bedfellows

H.V. (Doc) Evatt, former leader of the Australian Labor Party, was born at the Bank Hotel in East Maitland.

During its reign as the best accommodation in the Federal Territory, every prime minister of the time stayed at the Canberra Hotel at Yarralumla, ACT. The ALP's James Scullin stayed there while prime minister between 1929 and 1932, refusing the opulence of The Lodge. Other prime ministers to stay there include Billy Hughes, Arthur Fadden, Sir Robert Menzies, Harold Holt, Sir John Gorton and Sir Billy MacMahon, along with US war-hero General Douglas MacArthur. It closed as the Hotel Canberra in 1978 and was used briefly as an annexe to Parliament House, before its transformation into the first world-class hotel in the city. It was officially reopened by political combatants Sir John Gorton and Gough Whitlam in 1987.

At one time the biggest boarding-house in Canberra, the Kurrajong Hotel in Barton used to accommodate large numbers of public servants. Ben Chifley lived there during his term as prime minister from 1945 to 1949 and, as leader of the opposition in 1951, suffered a heart attack there and died.

It is said that Gough Whitlam popped the question to Margaret Dovey at the Florida Hotel in the Central Coast resort town of Terrigal.

Combatants of the 1970s and 1980s Malcolm Fraser and Bob Hawke stayed at the Canberra Rex Hotel often during those times. Hawke was ensconced here in damage control mode during the Whitlam dismissal and Iraqi loan crises in 1975.

The first week of the Hawke Government was administered from Noah's (now the Rydges Canberra) Hotel in Canberra while the new Prime Minister waited for an office.

The Paris Tavern in Melbourne's inner-suburban Brunswick was known as the R.J.L. Hawke Hotel during the late seventies and early eighties.

Canberra's Kingston Hotel was the venue for the '36 face-less men' incident. In March 1963, a photographer took a snap of ALP Leader, Arthur Calwell and Gough Whitlam standing outside this hotel, waiting for instructions whilst inside 36 unelected delegates were making decisions regarding the US Naval Bases in Western Australia during a special Labor Party Conference. The 'face-less men' phrase was coined by Robert Menzies, and the Liberal Party retained office in 1963 on the strength of this incident.

Liberal helpings

The traditon of pubs for Labor and clubs for Liberals was broken by Liberal leader and prime minister Malcolm Fraser's visit to Brisbane's Port Office Hotel during the 1983 election campaign. One of the bars was being renovated at the time, and Fraser offered to return and open the bar on its completion. He kept his word, and a gigantic piece of furniture in the beer garden was dubbed 'Mal's Seat'. The bar is now known as the PM's Bar, after Fraser thought the idea of calling it the Malcolm Fraser Bar 'too pompous'.

At the Canberra Rex Hotel Fraser plotted against Liberal leader Bill Snedden in 1975 and replaced him the following day. Fraser was later to be well remembered for a trouser-less episode in a Memphis, USA, hotel.

The Sydney Liar's Club in Flemington, Victoria, which opened in April 1991, was designed to be a tribute to the gross exaggeration and glorious lies told by Australia's politicians and bar-room drinkers. It includes life-size statues of Gough Whitlam, Sir John Kerr, and Malcolm Fraser (minus his trousers).

At the Deakin Inn in the ACT on 7 May 1989 the Liberal Party held a function during which Shadow Ministers Fred Chaney and Andrew Peacock advised John Howard that he was to be challenged for the leadership the following day. Unable to rally his supporters, Howard lost the leadership to Peacock the next day.

The Port Hotel at Carnarvon was taken over in 1958 by the future member for the seat of O'Connor, Wilson 'Ironbar' Tuckey, aged twenty-three. He also owned the Gascoyne Hotel in the same town, which was one of his last ventures before going into politics in 1980. Tuckey's nickname was said to have come about due to his strong-handed publican techniques.

Monday kind of Sunday

Publican of the Millaa Millaa Hotel in far northern Queensland, Bob McHugh, hosted a visit by premier Ted Theodore in 1922. A social event was organised for the Sunday night, but licensing regulations meant that liquor could not be served. But Theodore was a thinking (not to mention a drinking) man, and announced, 'As this is a Sunday evening when no liquor can be served on the premises, I therefore formally declare, for the purpose of the Licensing Act, that this day be Monday!'

The Shamrock Hotel in Stanley, Tasmania, became the Bay View Hotel, with its licensee being Michael Lyons, the grandfather of Joseph Lyons, history's only Tasmanian-born Prime Minister. The Billinudgel Hotel in NSW was the local for ex-National Party leader and deputy prime minister Doug Anthony.

Joh and Russ

Russell Hinze bought the Oxenford Tavern in 1983. A few months later Hinze, then Queensland's minister for main roads, was successful in having a service road and exit from the Gold Coast Highway built adjacent to his hotel.

The failed 1987 'Joh (Bjelke-Petersen, then Queensland premier) for Canberra' bid was launched at the Lakeside Hotel in Canberra by that state's branch of the National Party.

Devious acts

At the Queanbeyan Hotel during the second world war, a lieutenant and two sergeants of Dutch Indonesian origin, disaffected because their families had been left to the Japanese, planned to steal a bomber and fly home. They were incautious enough to trust another NCO, who betrayed them, and they were caught by the Dutch security authorities after trying to make contact with the Japanese from a room in the hotel. The two NCOs were tried in Ceylon and sentenced to twenty years, while the officer received a life sentence. A rumour at the time portrayed them as German infiltrators with a plan to blow up Government House.

The Canberra Rex Hotel in Braddon was used by an embassy for transmitting messages overseas in the 1960s.

ASIO officers were worried by a visit by the Yugoslav prime minister to the Lakeside Hotel in Canberra in 1973. They believed

Queanbeyan Hotel, Queanbeyan, NSW

terrorists could adulterate the air-conditioning with cyanide canisters. Their fears turned out to be unfounded.

On 21 April 1983 in the car-park of the former Nineteenth Hole Hotel in Narrabundah, Special Minister of State Mick Young warned a lobbyist of the impending deportation of Valerie Ivanov. That man was David Combe and he was told of tapes held by ASIO. Young resigned shortly after for leaking Cabinet secrets. Even though Prime Minister Hawke promised to stand by his long-term ally, he was forced to accept Young's resignation.

During a breakfast address by US President George Bush, surveillance equipment and cameras were hidden in the Capital Parkroyal Hotel's pot-plants.

Royalty

The Duke of Edinburgh stayed at the Castlemaine Hotel in Victoria in December 1867. The Duke and publican Lawrence Murphy played a game of billiards there, and Murphy was urged to lose by one the Duke's party. Murphy won, and promptly asked the Duke who was going to pay for the two bottles of champagne wagered on the outcome. The Royal obliged and the party continued well into the next morning.

The former Pic Nic Hotel in Sandringham, Victoria, became known as the Duke of Edinburgh before it was delicensed in the 1920s and converted into flats. One story goes that the change of name came about after the ubiquitous Duke stopped and had lunch at the hotel during his 1867 visit.

When the Queen of the Desert Hotel in Alice Springs was one year old (and known as the Gap) it hosted the Prince and Princess of

Wales on their 1983 tour. The royal couple and their entourage took up 25 rooms. But it was not the Princess's first visit to an Australian pub by any means. On 10 February 1981 Lady Diana Spencer enjoyed a drink at the Club House Hotel in Yass. A specially commissioned plaque is there to commemorate the event, nestled among prints of prize-winning Merino rams.

During the Queen's Coronation visit in 1954, her entourage dined at what was then known as the Grand Hotel in Wollongong, NSW, now Hal's Tavern.

The Queen and the Duke of Edinburgh dined at the former Alice Springs Hotel during the royal tour of 1963. This dinner received world-wide publicity when an exasperated Colonel Rose shouted to guests to 'shut-up' after the Territory Administrator, Roger Nott, had tried unsuccessfully to introduce the after-dinner speakers above the din. The Royal couple were not amused.

For some time there was a good natured feud between Arthur Elliot, the publican of the Broadway Hotel in New South Wales and the priest of St Barnabas Church opposite, Bob Forsyth. Each tried to outdo the other with slogans outside their institutions, but all was forgiven on St Barnabas' Day, when Father Bob served beers in the pub, and Arthur crossed the road to dole out free bread and wine.

Hobart's first Catholic chapel was set up in the Argyle Rooms of the former Carlton Castle Hotel by Father Therry until St Joseph's Church was built the following year.

In Broken Hill Catholics had their first mass at Finn's Hotel. This may have influenced their later impartial stand on the issue of temperance. Seventeen hotels closed in the Silver City due to the Local Option Polls of 1924, including the Athletic Club, Crystal, Oxford, Tramway, Crown and Anchor, Allendale, Cable, Wentworth and Reynolds'. The polls had been held in 1907, 1910 and 1913, with the voting going the way of licences being kept. In 1916 the hotels closed early, and in 1949 the Methodists discontinued their push for temperance. The closure of hotels at lunchtime on Sundays and the ban of bottled beer sales for that day was due to Paddy O'Neill, foundation president of the Barrier Industrial Council and a devout Catholic.

Toowoomba's former Imperial Hotel, since its demolition in 1971, has been the site of the Blessed Sacrament Shrine. This transformation from house of grog to house of god has happened at least three times. Tasmania's Queenstown Hotel is now used as the Salvation Army Citadel, and in 1901 the spectacular Osborne Hotel in Claremont, WA, and its equally spectacular site overlooking Freshwater Bay on the Swan River, were bought by the Catholic church and converted into a convent school, Loreto, now John XXIII College.

When the Lord Abbot of New Norcia, Western Australia, heard that dignitaries were visiting from Spain he started building a grand mission building.

Because of the Spanish Civil War the dignitaries never arrived, but the building was completed and became the Mission Hotel in 1954, after being used as a hostel for the Benedictine community in the town.

During the 1980s the Pyrmont Bridge Hotel in NSW was run by the 'Orange People' religious order, famous for its tenets of free love. The self-styled leader of the sect, Sri Bhagwan Ragneesh, died of AIDS in 1988.

St Pauls Tavern in Adelaide occupied the site of a beautiful old church. After the hotel closed in 1989, a $16.6 million dollar development was considered for the site, plans for which did not include the 130-year-old former church building. The state government would not pass an interim order preventing the demolition of the building, instead putting the onus on the Adelaide City Council. The building still stands.

A Baptist church for over 100 years before it was licensed, the Pulpit Tavern opened in Mount Barker, South Australia, in January 1991.

The Terowie Hotel in South Australia's north was originally a church. John Auer Mitchell ran a sly grog shop on the site before building the hotel and going legit in 1874. No wonder South Australians are happy for their capital to be known as the City of Churches.

The Man O'Ross Hotel in Ross, Tasmania stands on a corner of the main crossroads in the small Tasmanian township, and is known locally as Temptation. The other corner blocks are known as Recreation (the town hall); Salvation (the Catholic church); and Damnation (the old gaol, now gone).

5

The dry argument

For as long as pubs have dispensed their traditional brand of good cheer there have been those belonging to the Temperance movement who have toiled in vain to get publicans and their customers to 'see the light'. Some teetotallers have been moderately successful in limiting their community's access to the 'workingman's curse'.

 The Commercial Hotel in Swan Hill, Victoria, once hosted a meeting of the Temperance Society.

Camberwell

In the inner-city suburbs of Melbourne, especially in the streets of Richmond, Carlton, Collingwood and Fitzroy, there is a pub on almost every corner. It is hard to find a part of Melbourne without a pub – unless you go to Camberwell – a suburb with a population of over 100,000 people in Melbourne's affluent east. The irony is that the place itself is named after a pub, George Eastaway's Camberwell Inn, on the corner of what are now Burke and Riversdale Roads. Eastaway's hotel, built in the spring of 1853 in an area of the city that reminded him of Camberwell Green in his old home town of London, became

one of the major landmarks in the area. As the township grew, the surrounding district adopted the name of the hotel.

Hotels and inns played a large part in shaping the culture of the
Camberwell district – land auctions were held at Delany's Royal Hotel
(Canterbury Road was once named Delany's Road after the publican),
various lodges and public meetings were held in the Great Eastern
Hotel, and some of the various churches used hotels for services until
they had their own venues built.

It was these same churches, however, that rang the death knell
for Camberwell's pubs. People of non-conformist denominations
proliferated there (outnumbering Catholics four to one) and they
supported the Temperance movement that was sweeping the western
world. Local Option Polls were instigated in 1885, giving communities the chance to vote on the status of licences, and whether
to increase, decrease or keep the status quo. In Victoria the polls
closed around 1600 hotels, either directly or indirectly. In 1920, a
Local Option poll was held and two districts, Nunawading and
Booroondara, which became Camberwell, lost seven hotels, two wine
saloons and one spirits' grocers' licence by the end of that year.
Publicans of hotels such as Irwin's, Thorncombe, Long Hill, Survey
and Tyrone Hotels were granted £8600 compensation upon closure of
their business. Eventually even the Camberwell Hotel (previously the
Camberwell Inn) was demolished and replaced by a milk bar.

The Liquor Control Act of 1987, administered by the Liquor
Licensing Commission, requires a Local Option Poll to approve any
new 'on-licence' (hotel or full restaurant licence), and as recently as
1990 an application for a new reception house was rejected at a Local
Option Poll by nearly two to one.

During a local government shake-up in Melbourne during the mid-1990s the City of Camberwell ceased to exist. The prohibition in the area remained but whether or not it satisfies the Federal Government's anti-competition clauses is yet to be seen.

Although the people of Camberwell have been able to keep out the evil drink, the city has welcomed commercial sex services into their suburbs with the opening of the brothel 'Canterbury Tales' in recent years.

In Lilydale, Tasmania, the community didn't want a pub at all, and went as far as taking a prospective hotelier to the federal high court.

Even the might of Alan Bond couldn't get the licence through for his proposed Gap Tavern in Brisbane's western suburbs. After a 25-year local objection to the establishment of a hotel there it was eventually licensed on 11 November 1991 to Peter Quinn.

Thirstyville

Ever tried to do a pub-crawl around Canberra and not find any? Well, the truth is that they are everywhere but the Capital Territory has always had different liquor laws to other states and territories.

In 1915 the minister for home affairs, King O'Malley, issued an order that prohibition was to be enforced during the construction of the city. Canadian-born teetotaller O'Malley mounted the platform to press for prohibition in the 1880s and had associations with a temperance newspaper in Wichita, Kansas. For him, alcohol was 'stagger-juice'.

Soon after his arrival in Australia from America O'Malley entered parliament in South Australia (via Wangaratta and Melbourne) standing against a member of the strong Licensed Victualler's Party. O'Malley pulled the most votes, and had so influenced the female vote (at the polling booth for the first time) that he claimed it was the main reason for his win. At the next poll, in 1899, he was defeated by Charles Tucker, who had the misfortune to be the brother of an Adelaide hotelier. O'Malley immediately branded him a member of the 'stagger-juice brigade'.

O'Malley entered federal politics in 1901 in a Tasmanian seat. In 1915, as minister responsible for the construction of Canberra, he saw a golden opportunity to push his temperance values to the workers there, who drank in their tents but faced the danger of being sacked if they were caught. It was then that Canberra's sister city across the border in New South Wales, Queanbeyan, came into its own.

To the dismay of some of the Queanbeyan locals, their city became a sly-grog town when dozens of Canberra workers took to the streets, revelling in alcoholic nirvana. Queanbeyan hotels made a small fortune. Although the law prohibited the sale of alcohol in Canberra, it did not prohibit consumption, and bottles were brought across the border for friends, relatives and others, resulting in a considerable trade in empty bottles. Soon Canberra earned the nickname 'Thirstyville'.

However, when parliament came to the capital in 1927 members were served alcohol in a comfortable bar in Parliament House. Incensed at this, the workers, still trekking to Queanbeyan on Saturdays, pressed for a public vote on the issue.

The Bruce–Page Government approved a poll among residents in the ACT, giving them the options of prohibition of all liquor sales; no licences for hotels; open licences; or sales under government control. The population voted overwhelmingly for open licences, but the government took it upon itself to control the alcohol situation and, in addition to the three hotels it opened on 22 December 1928, it opened 'cafes' in empty shops in Civic, Kingston and Manuka.

This system was not a success, and the 'cafes' were described as 'no more than rudely furnished drinking shops'. The cafe at Manuka closed in 1930 due to lack of business, and the two others became notorious for dirt and drunkenness, earning the moniker of 'blood-houses'. The University College magazine described one: 'There were long dirty deal tables to hold the beer while the fights were on, and sawdust on the floor to soak up the blood . . . If you want ice-cream or tea and cakes, shun it; but if you want a pint of draught with a dash, then here you are!' The problem was so serious that in September 1933 Colonel Jones, superintendent of police, reported that of 55 charges of drunkenness the previous year, 46 had been associated with the cafes.

Things had changed by 1975 when the Territory's Liquor Act was introduced through federal parliament. Now any fit and proper person can apply for and receive a licence, providing that the premises comply with the guidelines presented by the ACT Liquor and Gaming Commission. This means that there is no real distinction between hotels, taverns, restaurants and nightspots, and the freedom of opening hours is the envy of many a bar in other cities. For this reason there are now very few premises calling themselves hotels in the city, but with over 500 places to buy a drink in Canberra, the Thirstyville nickname no longer applies.

While the Derrimut Hotel in Sunshine, Victoria, opened on 13 May 1929 to Mrs E. Fowler, the district's pioneering manufacturers H.V. McKay Pty Ltd (of Sunshine Harvester fame) vowed to fight the decision in the Licensing Court. A Local Option Poll found 614 votes for the licence and 550 against.

The curse of the working man

Ocean Grove, on the Bass Strait coast of Victoria, came into being as a model religious settlement under the direction of a Wesleyan minister, Reverend Osborne. An impressive coffee palace was built there in 1880, it had the outside appearance of a church. Methodist ministers bought up most of the proposed township's blocks, but the project eventually failed. The one legacy that Reverend Osborne left is his direction that the town be free of 'malted, vinous or spirited liquors'. However, Ocean Grove has grown to the extent that it now has a suburb, Collendina, and as Collendina is not considered to be Ocean Grove, the Collendina Hotel was built despite the good intentions of the reverend.

After protests by residents of Burnside, Adelaide, about plans to build a hotel in their suburb, they finally relented when the developers agreed to use the façade of a soon-to-be demolished bank as the front of the building. This proved too expensive, so the South Australian Brewing Company built a Georgian style hotel that looked like a bank on Glynburn Road. The Feathers certainly doesn't resemble the average pub.

Some teetotallers cannot even bear to look at a pub. The only municipal clock in the Essendon district for years was the one installed by Thomas Dern in October 1890 on the façade of his Moonee Ponds Hotel. Teetotallers complained about having to read the time from a clock on a hotel. In 1930 an electric clock was installed on the Essendon Town Hall.

Moonee Ponds Hotel, Moonee Ponds, Victoria

One businessman in Hobart, opposed to the sale of liquor, traded pints for pies when he turned the Queensborough Arms in Sandy Bay into a bakery.

In Adelaide, the country's first non-alcoholic tavern opened in the building that was the Old Rose Inn. The experiment failed.

The swill

Following a referendum in NSW on 10 June 1916 hotel bars were forced to shut their doors at 6 pm. This followed South Australia's lead and Victoria followed suit a few months later. It was the beginning of the dreaded 'six o'clock swill' that dominated the social life of many Australian men for the next four decades. Nearly 90 per cent of beer consumed in those times was between five and six in the afternoon.

The swill also had a profound effect on the design of hotels. Bars became choked late in the afternoon so walls were knocked out to extend them. Billiard rooms and large saloons became a luxury and were soon converted into drinking-halls. The counter top was cleared and linoleum and tiles became the preferred materials because they were easy to clean. The bottle trade flourished, and bottle departments were soon set up. The beginning of the end of the swill was when the liquor laws for licensed clubs were liberalised, though a referendum in NSW still voted overwhelmingly in favour of 'no change' to the closing times. A year later the laws were repealed in that state.

Going for gold

The Royal Hotel in Hill End, NSW, is the sole remaining hotel out of 50 that once traded in the goldrush town. It was built in 1872 and is classified by the National Trust. The main feature of the bar is a lithograph depicting Bernard Otto Holtermann. The work shows Holtermann advertising 'Holtermann's life-preserving drops' (nuggets of gold) while he stands next to the famous Holtermann Nugget that he found with another German, Alderman Beyers. Holtermann was known as a tyrant, scrooge and egotist, proclaiming himself the 'King of Hill End', but his nugget once held the world record for size and value.

During the boom years, a sweep of the bar-room floors of the Shamrock Hotel in Bendigo could net £4 a night in gold dust.

The Denver City Hotel in Coolgardie, Western Australia, is the only pub left in a town that in the golden days once had 26 of them. At one, the publican offered beer for only nine pence a glass. So many men came that they formed a queue stretching a couple of blocks. In local folk-lore it became known as Kennedy's Beer Day.

Boulder in WA was made up almost entirely of pubs during the early 1900s – the Boulder Block, Ivanhoe, Oraya, Burke's Perseverance and the Fimiston, to name a few, as well as a brewery. The pubs in Boulder provided drinks around the clock for the shift-working miners. Branded the 'dirty half acre' one block had eight pubs, but only the Boulder Block and Fimiston Hotels have survived. In mining the ground underneath the Boulder Block Hotel, one of the drives found its way into the hotel's cellar, which meant the miners could climb up to the bar through the cellar.

The Camp Hotel in Ballarat, Victoria, was built in 1861 on the site of the 'Little Engine' gold mine, which was where the first gold was found on the Western Plateau in 1856. Near the Camp Hotel, the Atlantic Hotel was situated on the No. 2 Band of Hope, the world's richest alluvial gold mine.

The Blarney Inn in Ballarat, Victoria, used to be called the Welcome Nugget

Hotel, in honour of the Welcome Stranger nugget, the second largest nugget ever found in Australia dug up directly opposite the hotel in 1888.

Sixteen-year-old Jim Larcombe struck his pick into the ground at Kalgoorlie and hit a solid submerged object. With his father, he extracted the 35.5 kilogram Golden Eagle nugget, so named because of its shape, and, to this date, the largest nugget found in Western Australia. It was sold to the Perth Mint to be melted down for ingots and Jim Larcombe Senior bought the Golden Eagle Hotel in Kalgoorlie with the profits.

Frequented by locals and hardy souls who try their luck panning for gold in the wild Highlands region of Victoria, the Kevington Hotel has been known for years as the 'Kevington Hilton', and there is more to the name than local pride. It seems that when the Melbourne Hilton was being built, one of the American directors of the hotel chain was taken to the district on a fishing trip. The party called in at the pub, and the American was so taken with it that he gave it the Hilton nickname. Apparently it wore the name on the roof, until Hilton management objected. But the locals know better.

The Aileron Hotel's first owner and builder was Fred Colson, a former cattle station owner who took part in the search for Harold Bell Lasseter, and the subsequent search for Hitchcock and Anderson, the lost searchers for Lasseter. The location of Lasseters Reef – a legendary vast lode of gold – remains a mystery to this day.

6

Pub culture

In the remote north-western corner of New South Wales is the two-pub town of Tibooburra. Its Family Hotel is one of the most unlikely settings for an art gallery. Originally built by Francis Bladen as the Tattersalls Hotel in 1882, on the walls here you will find works by eminent Australian artists Clifton Pugh and Russel Drysdale which will *never* leave the walls of the pub. It is not that the publican refuses to sell them – they are actually painted and sketched onto the walls. Drysdale, travelling through in 1970, was the instigator. His sketch, 'Old Timers', a study of local outback characters, is on the wall of the tap-room. The Australian pub had long been a source of inspiration for Drysdale – the Royal Hotel at Seymour in Victoria was the model for his classic painting 'Moody's Pub'.

About two years later Clifton Pugh was passing by Barney and Josh Davey's pub and spotted the Drysdale work. Around this time Barney had won first prize in a bareback riding competition, and Pugh painted Barney riding a maiden barebacked. Although the pub was closed that Sunday, a few more drinks were had, and some hand maidens were added. The problem with the mural, as the Daveys found out when they opened on Monday morning, was that Pugh had painted 'Bacchus' (Barney) naked, his penis hanging out for the world to see.

The Protestants of the town were most upset. The local policeman wandered by and decreed that the offending member must go, but the publican's wife said, 'If it's good enough for the Pope, it's good enough for the pub.' Eventually, the Daveys plucked a leaf from the mulberry tree growing in front of the post office, but the next hot day the glued-on leaf shrivelled to such an extent it really did look obscene.

During all this fuss the unfortunate local policeman drove the 400-mile return trip to Broken Hill to report to the city's police, who replied that they didn't want anything to do with the controversy. A fig leaf was eventually painted over Barney's penis.

When the pub was sold in June 1994, the asking price was just over $300,000, while the artwork alone has been valued at around $250,000. New publican Ian King is considering conservation measures to preserve the unique works for years to come.

A companion piece to the 'Bacchus' at Tibooburra holds pride of place at the Angaston Hotel in South Australia's Barossa Valley. Painted by local artist Timothy Messack in 1956, the mural is a reproduction of Rubens' famous 'Bacchus' with the main difference being the inclusion of likenesses of the publican's two children. The town's founder, George Fife Angas, was a noted wowser and would have turned up his heels at the erotic mural depicting Bacchus cavorting with maidens.

Better known to a multitude of Victorians (and indeed many Australians) as Young and Jackson's, the Princes Bridge Hotel is situated on perhaps Australia's best piece of real estate – the north-western corner of Swanston and Flinders Streets in central Melbourne. Once described as Victoria's only working goldmine, it is built on land bought for £100 by Melbourne's founder John Batman in 1837.

The hotel is best known as the home of the nude portrait 'Chloe'. The controversial painting was finished in 1876 by Chevalier Jules LeFebvre and won numerous medals including the Grand Medal of Honour and Melbourne's International Exhibition Gold Medal. It hung in the National Gallery despite objections from moralists who resented the 'indecent picture of a naked woman called by a classical name'. Bought by Henry Young for 880 guineas in 1908, 'Chloe' has hung in the Saloon Bar ever since.

'Chloe' went on tour during the first world war and raised £300 for the Red Cross. The prudish complaints were temporarily forgotten, although she was attacked by a drunken United States soldier on leave in 1943.

Prince's Bridge Hotel, Melbourne

Legend has it that LeFebvre used a beautiful but depressed Parisienne named Marie as his model for 'Chloe'. The story goes that one evening she gathered all her friends for a dinner party of startling magnificence. When the last of the guests had gone, she took a box of matches, boiled the heads, and then drank the poisonous water and collapsed.

There are many more pub nudes. The Union Club Hotel in Broken Hill features a painting of two nude blondes. Grong Grong's Royal Hotel is home to 'Chloe of the West'. A painting of an unnamed nude resting on a chaise-longue graces the public bar of the Shamrock Hotel in Alexandra, Victoria.

The highlight of the bar in the West Coast Hotel in Cooktown, far north Queensland, is a series of murals depicting life on the early Palmer River goldfields. They were painted by Sydney artist Garnett Agnew, who had worked for the *Bulletin* in the 1930s. Payment for the artwork was enough rum or beer to keep him in trim while the murals were being painted. The last mural has a wall to itself and features several of the locals in a party scene.

Heidelberg and a piss-take

When it was first established, the Old England Hotel in Heidelberg, Victoria, was set amongst idyllic scrubland, and was the subject of many paintings by the Heidelberg School of artists. The Heidelberg School itself, at nearby Eaglemont, spawned the Australian Impressionist movement, with the major painters being Tom Roberts, Arthur Streeton, Fred McCubbin and Charles Conder. Another famous local

artist was Walter Withers, who painted 'The Selector's Home' and the award-winning 'Tranquil Winter and Evening in Heidelberg'. The setting then was considered an ideal one for the romantic eye of the impressionists who all frequented the hotel, especially Streeton, Conder and Roberts.

The foyer of the Parmelia Hilton Hotel in Perth is graced by two Sidney Nolan originals, and also a mirror from Italian dictator Benito Mussolini's palace. The hotel was named after the vessel *Parmelia*, the first ship to carry settlers to Perth. Pride of place in the hotel's Adelphi Beer Hall is given to a reproduction of the famous Belgian 'Mannikin Piss' statue. Legend has it that when a rich Brussels merchant's son went missing he pledged to build a statue for the city depicting the boy as he was found. The lad was found relieving himself in a canal.

The three pubs in Normanton, Queensland – the Central, Albion and National – were known simply as the Blue, Yellow and Purple hotels after a community-organised spruce up of the townscape.

In a town with a population of just eleven, you need to have a pub that stands out, brings travellers through the door, and has something that makes them want to stay. The Broad Arrow Tavern in the town of the same name, 38 kilometres north of Kalgoorlie, is famous locally for its graffiti. You can see the musings of travellers on the doors, walls, and even ceilings.

Get this down, can you?

It is likely that prominent writers Will Gillespie, Henry Lawson and 'Breaker' Morant all quenched their thirst at the Enngonia (now Oasis) Hotel in Enngonia, north-western NSW. As they were all in the district – Gillespie and Morant on stations and Lawson tramping his way to Hungerford – it is possible that they may have been inspired by Captain Starlight, who held up the hotel and shot a policeman. Or by bushranger Harry Law, whose final resting-place was the hotel.

Morant was a show-off. At the Exchange Hotel in Parkes, NSW, one of the earliest hotels and the largest in the district, he leapt on to his horse and cleared a six-foot high brick wall at midnight. Further north at the Barwon Inn in Walgett Morant rode his horse into the hotel, then accepted and won a wager to jump a stout, high wire fence at the side of the road. His horse cleared it with a leap that left him seven yards clearance on the far side.

James Dennis was licensee of the Auburn Hotel in Auburn, South Australia, from 1865 to 1877. His son, the writer C.J. Dennis, was born there on 7 September 1876. Speaking of Dennis, the hotel at Bulleen in Melbourne's east was once called the Sentimental Bloke Hotel after his most famous poem, but is now the plain old Manningham Hotel.

While laid up at the Caledonian Inn in Robe, South Australia, in 1862 after a fall from a horse, poet Adam Lindsay Gordon met and married Margaret Park, the inn-keeper's daughter. A pub also saw his demise when he shot himself amongst the ti-trees out the front of the Marine Hotel in the Melbourne bayside suburb of Brighton. The hotel's lounge bar, known as the Adam Lindsay Gordon Lounge, was opened on the centenary of his death in 1970.

Marine Hotel, Brighton, Victoria

A more contemporary poet, Dame Edna Everage, wrote a poem specially for the re-opening, in 1987, of the Earl of Aberdeen Hotel in Adelaide. Her 'Ode to the Earl' went something like this . . .

> *And so upon this gorgeous day,*
> *so sunny and serene*
> *we salute the transformation*
> *of the Earl of Aberdeen*
> *Since the far off eighteen fifties*
> *a modest pub was there*
> *but now it's come into its own,*
> *the pride of Hurtle Square!*

Kylie Tennant's novel *Tiburon* was written at the Canowindra Hotel, Western NSW, when her husband worked at the local school. Further west, the author of *I Can Jump Puddles*, Alan Marshall, spent some time at the now delicensed Homebush (later Paika Run) Hotel at Penarie.

Apart from being Dawn Fraser's pub, the Riverview Hotel in Balmain was also famous as a haven for a writers' group known as the 'Stenhouse Circle' (David Williamson was a member) who used to meet there in the early 1980s.

Demolished in the late 1950s, the Swanston Family Hotel in Melbourne was a writers' headquarters between the 1930s and 1950s. Painters, musicians, philosophers and historians also gathered there, under the guidance of Brian Fitzpatrick. Among the writers to be seen and heard there were Judah Waten, Jack Stevenson, Alan Davies, Chris Wallace-Crabbe, and Germaine Greer – members of the 'Melbourne Push'.

Samuel Clemens, better known as American writer Mark Twain, worked at Melbourne's old Menzies Hotel in Bourke Street as a stoker, shovelling the coal in the basement to feed the furnaces. He had in fact asked if he could stoke the fires as part of a fitness regimen. Clemens also stayed at Horsham's White Hart Hotel in 1898, and wrote about the hotel in his book *More Tramps Abroad*, in which he mentions the street-side greenery of the town.

Pubs have long been settings for Australian stories. Some of the many that come to mind are the Post Office Hotel in Julia Creek, Queensland in Neville Shute's *A Town like Alice*; the Belmont Hotel at Belmont and Inlet Hotel at Airey's Inlet, both on Victoria's south-western coast, in Arthur Upfield's *Boney* detective series; the Warrnambool Hotel in Frank Hardy's *Yarns of Billy Borker*; the Ocean

Beach at Perth's suburban Cottesloe, which features as the 'Seaview Hotel' in Robert Drewe's *The Body Surfers*. The Lands Office Hotel (now Tavern) in Brisbane was described in David Malouf's *Johnno* as the 'least rowdy of all of Brisbane's pubs'. The Nedlands Park Hotel (or Steve's) in suburban Perth is the subject of Hal Colebatch's poem 'Saturday afternoon at the Nedlands Hotel'.

John Pascoe Fawkner was not only publican of the first hotel built in Melbourne, the Royal, in 1837, but he also started Melbourne's first newspaper there. He published the *Port Phillip Gazette* in a hand-written format. The building also doubled as the city's first lending library, where overseas books and papers were available without charge to guests and at a small charge for others.

The Grand Hotel on Thursday Island, situated opposite the wharf where the Horn Island Ferry berths, was a haunt of writer Somerset Maughan. The building burned down in 1993.

Western writer Zane Gray stayed at the Pacific Hotel in Cairns during his running battles with the big fish in the Coral Sea, and also at Watsons Bay Hotel in Sydney.

The John Barleycorn Hotel in Collingwood (now the Bagdad) was named after Robbie Burns' poem 'Ballad of Brewing', which went like this:

> John Barleycorn was a hero bold
> Of noble enterprise
> For if you do but taste his blood
> Twil make your courage rise!

The suburb also has a hotel named after the Scottish wordsmith.

Eminent journalist E.G. 'Dry-Blower' Murphy lived at the Shaftsbury Hotel in Perth for most of the years that he contributed his column 'Verse and Worse' to the *Sunday Times*. It appeared each Sunday from 1907 to 1938.

The Ettamogah Pub at Table Top near Albury, NSW, opened in 1982 after a concept conceived by artist Ken Maynard, who had drawn a popular comic strip of the same name for the *Australasian Post* for over twenty years. Husband-and-wife team Lindsay and Sonia Cooper decided to build the lop-sided pub with the Chevy Ute on the roof and all the assorted road-signs and drunken animals made famous by the cartoon. A franchise, which saw another Ettamogah Pub built on Queensland's Sunshine Coast in 1984, was put up for sale so that the concept could be built overseas.

Celluloid heroes

The Australian pub has been seen in many movie productions, some more successful than others. *Ned Kelly*, starring Mick Jagger, was filmed in part at the Royal Mail Hotel in Braidwood, NSW. The Royal Hotel in Binnaway, NSW, was the setting for the fight scene in *The Shiralee*.

The Royal Hotel in Nimmitabel, in the southern highlands of NSW, was used in the classic Australian film, *The Sundowners* (as the 'Australian') and later became a motel. One of the stars of that film, Doris Goddard (who became Doris Bishop) also became a publican. She had starred in films alongside such luminaries as Katherine Hepburn, Robert Mitchum, Peter Ustinov and Bob Hope. Doris named her pub in Surry Hills, NSW, the Hollywood Hotel.

'Chips' Rafferty, the famous Australian actor, was a regular at the bar of the Mansions Hotel in Kings Cross, NSW, and a noted practical joker. One of his favourite pranks was to pinch drinkers' beers and place them on the overhead ledge, at least eight feet above the ground. Poet Christopher Brennan also held court at the Mansions.

The Harbour View Hotel at Miller's Point, NSW, was used as the location for the movie *Starstruck*, which included an all-in dance shuffle on top of the unusually shaped bar. Also in Sydney, the Imperial Hotel in Erskineville was featured in *The Adventures of Priscilla – Queen of the Desert* and hosts a drag show on weekends as a tribute to the successful film. Mario's Palace in Broken Hill also featured in the film.

Alfred Hitchcock's nephew once visited the Babinda Hotel in far north Queensland to assess it as a location for a proposed film of Colleen McCullough's *The Thorn Birds*. The book was eventually turned into a mini-series, and the Babinda Hotel lost its shot at stardom.

Some Queensland hotels *have* made the leap onto celluloid. The Country Life Hotel in Kin Kin on Queensland's Sunshine Coast featured in the movie *Silent Reach*, an early James Bond-type movie, and was also used in a XXXX cricket commercial. The Federal Hotel at McKinlay in outback western Queensland was the pub featured in *Crocodile Dundee*. It quickly changed its name to the Walkabout Creek Hotel. Set amongst beautiful mango trees, the Kuttabul Hotel in north Queensland was once a picture theatre.

South Australian pubs have also benefited from the film industry. The Macclesfield Hotel in the Adelaide Hills became the 'Railway Arms' for the street scenes in the South Australian Film Corporation's *Weekend of Shadows*. And filming began in January 1993 at the Portland

Hotel, Port Adelaide, for another South Australian Film Corporation production, *Bad Boy Bubby*, a film about a young misfit and a rock-and-roll band. This hotel was chosen out of 15 considered in the docks area for the film that won the Best Australian Film at the 1994 Australian Film Industry Awards.

The Hotel St Moritz in St Kilda was originally the Wattle Path Dance Hall, opened in 1923. It then became a movie studio owned by F.W. Thring (father of star actor, Frank), known as Efftee Film Productions. Some of the early George Wallace films were made there, and Charles Chauvel hired the facilities there on numerous occasions. One of the first films made was *A Ticket in Tatts*. It was later used as an ice-skating rink, one of two in Melbourne. Auctioned in December 1980, the Builder's Labourers Federation banned further destruction of the building after Whelan the Wrecker had started work. The building burnt down in mysterious circumstances on 22 September 1982, leaving just the façade, but reopened under the management of French accommodation group Accor in 1991 as the Novotel.

On the box

Many directors of shows produced for television in this country, both drama and comedy, turn to the pub as a set to add colour and realism. Regular viewers would have seen the Retreat Hotel in Abbotsford, Victoria, in *The Sullivans*; the Chateau Commodore Hotel in Melbourne in *The Box*; the Club Hotel in Minyip, Victoria as Vic Buckley's hotel in *The Flying Doctors*; and the Bland Hotel in Quandialla, NSW, which featured in the ABC's war epic, *1915*. An episode of the popular British TV series *Minder* was set at the Somerset Hotel in Sydney's

73

inner-suburb Redfern. Mulcahy's Hotel in North Melbourne was the location for the bar-room brawl scene for failed Australian film *The Brown-out Murders* about an American serial killer's deeds in Melbourne during the second world war.

Actors spend plenty of time in pubs, so why not turn one into a television station? That was the fate of the former Queens Hotel in Townsville, built in 1873 and a National Trust and Australian Heritage Commission listed building, now occupied by North Queensland Telecasters Pty Ltd.

In Glebe in Sydney's inner-west, the Australian Youth Hotel was known to workers at the nearby Channel 10 television studio as 'Studio 11', and just across Blackwattle Bay, the now demolished Warwick Castle Hotel in Balmain, hosted television personality Lenore Smith of *Flying Doctors* fame, who had her christening party there.

You may have seen the advertisements for XXXX beer that feature the lonely outback-scape of the Royal Mail at Hatfield, NSW.

Break a leg!

The first Australian theatrical production was staged at a hotel, at one end of a bar-room converted into a temporary stage. The appropriately named play, *The Hotel*, was first enjoyed by the public in 1796 at Robert Sidaway's Chequers Hotel.

The first permanent home of the stage in this country was in the saloon of the now long-gone Royal Hotel in Sydney's George Street. Barnett Levey was thought to have opened the theatre there after he planned to convert his windmill and warehouse into a hotel – a development that sparked heated arguments with Governor Ralph Darling.

When Darling returned to England, Levey continued with his renovations and, with the consent of the newly appointed Governor Bourke, opened a theatre in a big room of his hotel. The only problem was that all the plays performed there had to be licensed in England by the Lord Chamberlain. Nevertheless, on 26 December 1832 Levey treated the Sydney public to *Black-ey'd Susan*, followed by *Monsieur Tonson* and *Fortune's Frolic*. Funds were raised by benefit musical concerts, and the struggling Levey made an absolute success of his venture. The Theatre Royal, another project of Levey's, was established in July of the following year, and the Royal Hostel was no longer used for this sort of entertainment.

The British and American Hotel in Bendigo hosted American actress Lola Montez while she was on a goldfields tour in the 1860s. Montez was so taken with Sandhurst (as Bendigo was then known) that she bought a house there and hoped to settle eventually in Australia.

As the Hotel Victoria, the Theatre Royal Hotel in Brisbane first opened in 1863 when G.B. Mason produced the first concert there. Mason opened his concert hall two years later, which was soon known as the Queensland Theatre. On 18 April 1881, after renovations to the old theatre, the Theatre Royal was born. Performers including George Wallace senior and junior, Roy Rene, Buster Fiddess, Bobby Limb, Barry Crocker and Toni Lamond appeared at the Theatre Royal. The last performance was on 12 December 1959. The building was used for a succession of nightclubs until its demolition.

More lately, the Bank Hotel in Newtown in Sydney's inner south has hosted plays, including in 1992 the award-winning *To*, by Jim Cartwright. The setting for this play was originally a Northern England pub.

The first original play to be written and presented in Australia, the Samson Company's production of *The Bandit of the Rhine* by Evan Henry Thomas, was performed at Launceston's British Hotel in October 1835.

The barmen at Jimmy Richardson's Australia Felix Hotel on the corner of Bourke and Russell Streets in Melbourne were well trained. There would be a rush between acts at the theatre when the barmen would 'line 'em up' at the sound of the bell, rung at the end of each act.

We drink in moderation . . .

The Town & Country Hotel in Sydney's southern suburb St Peters, was the main inspiration for the Slim Dusty hit 'Duncan'. After trying to sell Duncan Urquhart a life insurance policy, a frustrated Pat Alexander gave up, and Duncan suggested a beer at this pub. Alexander wrote the song and the rest is history. Slim did have a beer with Duncan at the Town & Country as part of the publicity for the song.

Like the disagreement over which is the oldest pub in the country, two pubs in separate states have squabbled over the dubious honour of being the original 'Pub with no Beer'. The confusion apparently stems from the fact that there was a poem of that name as well as a song. The poem was written by Dan Sheehan about the time that American soldiers, on R&R after the Battle of the Coral Sea, drank dry the Day Dawn Hotel in Ingham, Queensland. This pub, which became Lee's, was the recipient of a Bicentennial Commonwealth grant for a plaque heralding its fame as the Pub with no Beer.

Forty years later balladeer Gordon Parsons begged to differ. He

The Pub With No Beer, Taylor's Arm, NSW

claimed that he wrote the song – which became known as Slim Dusty's signature tune – in the late 1950s after being given one verse of Sheehan's original poem. The pub Parsons wrote about, the Cosmopolitan at Taylor's Arm, NSW, changed its name to The Pub with no Beer, even though there wasn't a thirsty punter in sight. Gordon Parsons died in 1990 and has been imortalised in Tamworth's Walk of Fame. Sheehan, who died in 1977 aged 95, is regarded the poet laureate of the cane-cutting town of Ingham.

Slim Dusty, the recipient of Australia's first-ever gold record, for the song, remains diplomatic. 'Dan's is a fine poem,' he said during an interview for the *Australiasian Post*, 'but Gordon's is a better song.'

Harold Ramsey's claim to fame is that it was he who first sang

A.B. Paterson's 'Waltzing Matilda' in public. He gave his performance at the North Gregory Hotel in Winton, western Queensland. The song was written at Combo Waterhole near there in 1895.

Country and western singer Stan Coster's song named after the Wobbly Boot Hotel in Boggabilla, northern NSW, is less well-known.

Musical moments

Australian musical entertainment as a permanent fixture started at Sydney's Clown Hotel in 1844, when the hotel was owned by a recently arrived thespian and impresario, George Coppin, who had played the Royal Victoria Theatre. Patrons sang along to a pianist and conductor.

William Vincent Wallace, while on a visit to Tasmania in 1838, was so captivated by the picturesque setting of New Norfolk's Bush Inn that he conceived the theme 'Scenes that are Brightest'. It was incorporated into the opera *Maritana*, first performed in London in 1854. The opera was produced and broadcast from the New Norfolk's Bush Inn on national radio station 7ZL in 1932. Dame Nellie Melba sang from *Maritana* during her farewell visit to the island in 1924, when she also stayed at the New Norfolk's Bush Inn.

In 1881 the International Hotel in Port Pirie, South Australia, hosted performances of the Royal English Opera Company.

Now gone, the Commercial Hotel in Wangaratta, Victoria, hosted musicians and actors – including Melba – when they performed at Her Majesty's Theatre next door.

The Rathdowne Tavern in Melbourne's Carlton was formerly

known as Melba's Tavern. Another hotel, in the Western Tasmanian hamlet of Leslie, was named the Madame Melba for four years.

 Formerly known as Carlyon's, the Esplanade Hotel in St Kilda, Victoria, boasted a nationally famous orchestra.

Good gigs

Pop and rock music are indebted to the hotels and bars of Australia. When the legal drinking age was lowered in the late sixties rock music made the shift from town halls and RSL clubs to hotel lounge rooms. Bands like Billy Thorpe and the Aztecs and later AC/DC, Cold Chisel and The Angels were at the vanguard of the pub rock scene. Australia was at the forefront of this movement.

Some pub venues have become legendary. The Cricketers' Arms Hotel in Richmond, Victoria, is where Grammy-award winning Australian pop band Men at Work got their start in the late 1970s. The Largs Pier in Adelaide was one of the first venues for popular Australian rock act Cold Chisel, who later immortalised another hotel, the ill-fated Star Hotel in Newcastle West, on their album 'East'. Midnight Oil played some scorching sets at Narrabeen's Royal Antler Hotel (now Narrabeen Sands) and Melbourne's Hunters and Collectors recorded their 'Way To Go Out' record and video at the Prince of Wales Hotel in St Kilda, sadly no longer a live venue. The Lansdowne and Annandale Hotels in Sydney's inner west have also gone the same way, but these decisions are part and parcel of the change of a hotel's function. Now the lounge bars of some pubs pulsate to hip-hop, techno, jungle, and drum and bass music, as far removed from disco as opera!

Blood on the wattle

One of the bloodiest battles ever at an Australian hotel was Milperra, or the Father's Day Massacre on 2 September 1989 in Sydney. The Commancheros and the Bandidos, rival biker gangs, had a battle in the car-park during a bike part swap-meet. A feud, allegedly over territories of drug distribution networks, had been brewing since the Bandidos broke away from the Commancheros. The melee, involving baseball bats, machetes, handguns, shotguns and hunting rifles, claimed the lives of seven people – Commancheros 'Leroy' Jeschke, 'Foghorn' Lane, 'Dog' McCoy and 'Sparrow' Romcek, and Bandidos 'Shadow' Campbell and 'Chopper' Cianter. Fifteen-year-old Leanne Walters was killed by a stray bullet and 21 people were injured. In a committal hearing held under intense security, 43 men were charged with seven counts of murder each.

As the Home from Home Hotel, Hannan's Hotel in Kalgoorlie was the scene of a race riot on the Australia Day long weekend of 1934. On the Sunday, an Italian barman ejected an Australian from his hotel. The unfortunate man hit his head on the gutter and died of a fractured skull. This incident ignited the simmering tension between Italian and Anglo-Saxon mining communities, and the next evening a congregation of miners gathered. A night of violence followed, including an attempt to burn down the hotel. The mob eventually moved on to the Kalgoorlie Wine Saloon and looted and vandalised it before setting it alight. The inferno brought firemen and police. Two days later, every 'foreign' business in Kalgoorlie and Boulder had been either looted or gutted. Worst hit were the All Nations Hotel in Kalgoorlie, and the Cornwall, Main Reef and International Club Hotels in Boulder. Several people were badly injured, and two Australians and a man of Slavic origin were killed. The police were criticised for leaving the rioters as long as they did, while they maintained that they were waiting for the situation to burn itself out. The Kalgoorlie Wine Saloon is now a restaurant, and the All Nations Hotel has been demolished.

At 12.42 in the morning of 13 February 1978, a bomb exploded in a garbage bin at the George Street entrance of the Sydney Hilton, killing council workers Alex Carter and William Favell and policeman Paul Birmistriw. Strangely, no one claimed responsibility for what was presumed to be Australia's first taste of international terrorism. Police suspected that members of a religious sect called Ananda Marga were responsible. In one of the most bizarre investigations in the history of policing in Australia, suspect Tim Anderson was arrested and acquitted twice. Anderson's accuser, public servant Evan Pederick, was sentenced to twenty years for his assumed part in the crime. There is still talk of a conspiracy involving Australia's Secret Service organisations and the Army, but this has never been proved.

One of the most famous riots in Australian pub history coincided with the closing of the Star Hotel in Newcastle West on 19 September 1979. The hotel had become run-down in the years before its closure, and its fate was

Sydney Hilton, Sydney, NSW

sealed when Tooths Hotels sold the building to the Hooker Corporation for redevelopment.

The pub was a gathering place for the city's disenfranchised youth. Alex Duff, in a letter to the editor of the *Newcastle Morning Herald* on the morning of the riot, summed up what it meant to the kids. 'The young people of Newcastle have been struck a body blow by the decision to close down the Star Hotel,' he wrote. On the last trading night, a gig was organised with bands Meccalissa and Heroes on the bill. A crowd gathered from about 4 pm, and over the next five hours swelled to perhaps 7000. The night was largely incident-free until 10 o'clock, when Heroes finished their set.

Suddenly police swarmed the venue and Heroes' lead singer, Peter deJong, was allegedly hit in the mouth with his own microphone stand. The crowd became incensed by the police presence and, whatever the catalyst, the hotel erupted and violence came to King Street in a big way. An unmarked police car was overturned and set alight, a 'paddy-wagon' was burnt – with a man trapped inside – and the firemen trying to put out the fires were pelted with rocks and bottles. The firemen eventually extinguished the fracas by turning their hoses on the rioters.

Fourteen police and eight pub-goers were injured; 29 people were charged with nearly 100 different offences.

The community was outraged. Premier Neville Wran and opposition leader John Mason politicised the incident. Letters to the editor of the *Newcastle Herald* offered opinions for a week. Youth unemployment was the Steel City's most contentious issue. Songwriter Don Walker penned the song 'Star Hotel', which was recorded by his band, Cold Chisel, who used it as the theme for their 'Youth in Asia' tour. 2JJ Radio presenter Marius Webb recorded the Cold Chisel show for posterity. When asked whether the Star had been replaced in the hearts of Newcastle's youth, he replied: 'Not to my mind. I think that it's interesting that a place like the Star, which may well have died of its own accord in a few years, went down in flames because an outside agency decided to ignore community opinion and obey the laws of Mammon rather than listen to the locals about their needs. The Star filled an unusual niche in Newcastle's social environment precisely because it was unique. I've been in dozens of other pubs around the country that share elements of what the Star provided but none other has had the rather mysterious combination of them as at the Star.'

Five thousand army troops stationed at Casula Camp in NSW in 1916 were told they were to accept a new training regimen that involved an extra one-and-a-half hours a day. For some, this meant a straight shift of twenty-seven hours, so the troops decided to strike. On 14 February the leaders of the strike, well-primed with drink, led a contingent of men to storm the camp liquor stores. Taking every bottle, they set out for Liverpool where they attacked the Lachlan Macquarie Hotel (then known as the Golden Fleece). Then they did over the Commercial Hotel, causing damage worth nearly £2000. The NSW Cabinet issued an edict that all pubs should shut for the day. The soldiers continued their rampage, boarding trains to the city, where they faced military police at Central Station. Shots were fired, killing one soldier and injuring seven others. The chaos continued, terrifying members of the public, who eventually turned their wrath on the publicans. The Prohibition movement was growing steadily, and the riot was the perfect excuse for a push towards restrictions of opening hours for hotels.

7

Guests of
Her Majesty's Hotel

The hotel is a haven for good, hard-working men but occasionally pubs can attract a more undesirable sort of clientele.

Squizzy

In January 1908, 20-year-old Joseph Theodore Leslie Taylor, better known as 'Squizzy', robbed the Cherry Tree Hotel in Richmond, Victoria of ten shillings. He was caught and sent to jail after giving cheek to the bench. Taylor went on to dominate Melbourne's underworld, his nefarious pursuits included gambling, blackmail, intimidation and murder. He would alternate between being friend and foe to publicans, but was a popular figure around Richmond, once describing himself as only a 'newspaper hero'.

Taylor was often seen in the company of SP bookie, Jack Corry, and former rogue mayor, Con Loughnan, and he would cruise the streets of Richmond, waving at his loyal subjects from his chauffeur-driven Stutz. His luck ran out in 1927 when he was shot dead in a house in Carlton.

One famous licensee of Hallam's Road Hotel in Victoria was a Mrs Bufford, Taylor's sister. He visited there often, as he did the Corryong Hotel on the Victorian side of the Murray River border with New South Wales. Taylor reportedly made a killing (metaphorically) while in the town for the race meeting. He has even had a hotel named after him. Established in the 1850s in the Melbourne suburb of Fitzroy, Squizzy Taylor's Hotel opened as the Leviathan, and was more recently known as the Renown Hotel.

Running a pub can be murder

Publicans have been both murder victims and perpetrators. William Graham of the defunct Balranald Inn, NSW; Stanley Young of the Mount Warning Hotel in Uki, NSW; William Brown of the Peninsula Hotel, Mandurah, WA; and Martin Shanahan of Dubbo's Macquarie Inn all met their makers behind the bars of their hotels.

Publican of Rockhampton's Golden Age Hotel, an M. Halligan, was ambushed on his way back from the gold-diggings and three men were charged with murder. Halligan's inn was itself described as a 'nursery for villains', from which they graduated from horse-thieving to bushranging and murder.

The first person to be lynched in South Australia was caught in the Rob Roy Hotel in Adelaide. His punishment was dealt out in nearby Hurtle Square.

A dangerous hotel was the Squatter's Home at Salt Creek on South Australia's Coorong. The pub existed from 1847 to 1877 under various names, including the Overlander, Traveller's Rest, and Salt Creek Tavern. The story goes that after one licensee, Will Robinson, was murdered, his widow married the prime suspect in the investigation, Malachai Martin. The identity of Robinson's murderer was never determined, but Martin was tried and hanged for another murder in 1862.

A sleeping mother and daughter died in a fire at the Isisford Hotel (formerly Imperial) in Western Queensland in September 1956. It was later proved that the fire was deliberately lit. Frederick Aitcheson of the Club Hotel and Kevin Johnson of the Golden West Hotel were charged with arson and murder and given long sentences.

> At the former Racecourse Hotel in Longford, Tasmania in the 1800s, a harvest hand placed two gold sovereigns on the bar, with the intention of shouting the bar. For some reason a young woman standing nearby decided to swallow them. Men at the bar then killed her by hitting her on the head with a bottle and cut her up in search of the coins. Three men were hanged on a nearby hill for their part in the murder.

Drugs in the family

On the evening of Friday 15 July 1977, anti-drugs campaigner Donald Mackay was executed in the car-park of the Griffith Hotel in rural NSW. His influence was starting to have an effect on the operations of 'La Famiglia', co-ordinators of a Griffith-based drug distribution ring headed at the time by Robert Trimbole. Mackay's body has never been found.

James Frederick Bazley was finally arrested on the basis of testimony of 'The Songbird', Gianfranco Tizzoni, who had contracted Bazley to kill Mackay on behalf of Trimbole. Bazley was sentenced to life imprisonment at Melbourne's Pentridge Gaol on 16 April 1986.

Trimbole and Tizzoni plotted another murder in March 1979, at the Westmeadows Tavern in Melbourne's outer northern suburbs. Bazley was to ply his trade and remove the threat of former 'Mr Asia' drug couriers turned police informants, Douglas and Isobel Wilson.

The Britannia Hotel (now the Brendan Behan) at Chippendale, NSW was the last drinking place of alleged heroin dealer Warren Lanfranchi, who was shot dead by Detective Roger Rogerson in nearby Dangar Place. Rogerson had been linked with Arthur Stanley 'Neddy' Smith and Bill Duff, of the Iron Duke Hotel at Alexandria, where Smith was lucky to survive an attempted hit-and-run incident. Smith allegedly also had links to the fire-bombing of the Lansdowne Hotel in nearby Darlington.

The Water Rat Hotel in South Melbourne gained notoriety when, as the Druid's, it was the scene of the slaying of Federated Painters and Dockers Union Secretary, Patrick Shannon, in October 1973. People

Lansdowne Hotel, Darlington, NSW

say that his ghost that haunts the cellar. Bill 'The Texan' Longley, a one-time minor US presidential candidate, was later convicted of Shannon's murder.

In 1973, the tension between factions of the Federated Painters and Dockers Union touched Fitzroy in Melbourne when docker Laurence Chamings and Nicholas Kolovrat, a ten-year-old boy, were killed by a gunman who burst into the Moonee Valley Hotel.

With friends like prison escapee Peter Robert Gibb and prison officer-turned-fugitive Heather Parker, Archie Butterly didn't need any enemies. After their escape from the Melbourne Remand Centre in March 1993, the three made their way to the Gaffney's Creek pub in eastern Victoria. Two days later, following a shoot-out with the police, Gibb and Parker were captured, but Butterly's body was found some time later. Police confirmed that he had died under suspicious circumstances.

Fire!

Way out west Robert McAllister took over the Carnarvon Hotel on 26 May 1912, and that very night it burnt to the ground. Investigators declared there were no suspicious circumstances. Later, in 1926, McAllister took over the Port Hotel. It was ablaze within two weeks. Miraculously, the temporary bar was saved, possibly due to firemen taking a keen interest in its survival. McAllister then took over the Settler's Hotel on 27 February 1927 and within hours it burnt to the ground and was never rebuilt. McAllister went back to manage the Port Hotel when it was rebuilt – it mustn't have been combustible.

The London Hotel near Warri Homestead in the Ariah Park district of the New South Wales Riverina, was built in the 1860s. One story goes that on a shearing shed cut-out the publican and his wife, after drinking with the lads, were locked in a small room while the shearers ransacked the place.

'Shanghai'

The famous wedge-shaped Hero of Waterloo Hotel in Miller's Point, Sydney, had a smugglers' tunnel that ran 150 metres through solid sandstone to Darling Harbour. It was a favoured location for the 'shanghai-ing' of sailors. At times extra crew were needed for the ships in Sydney Cove and Darling Harbour, and the standard recruitment practice was to ply a young man with enough alcohol to ensure that he passed out at some stage during the night. He usually woke to a hangover suddenly made much worse by sea-sickness.

At the Pier Hotel in Bunbury, Western Australia, in November 1918, Australia's last 'shanghai' occurred. In this case, the S.S. *Monkbarns* found itself a sailor short. An unfortunate Norwegian man was plyed with grog until he passed out, bundled into a rowboat, taken to the vessel anchored a mile-and-a-half off-shore, and thrown into a bunk in the ship's forecastle. The unwilling seaman brought an unsuccessful law suit against the Master, Captain Jock Donaldson, on arrival in Cape Town. There's no justice for a drunken sailor.

Payback

Matilda's Tavern in Queen Street, Melbourne, is in the basement of the former Victoria Club building that was the venue for one of Australia's most daring unsolved crimes – the 1976 Great Bookie Robbery. No charges have ever been laid, and the bookmakers to this day are coy about how much money was really stolen, but it was almost certainly millions more than reported. The robbery sparked war between jealous rival factions, with at least four suspects dying violently.

The slaying of alleged standover man Brian Kane at the Quarry Hotel in East Brunswick in November 1992 was one in an extraordinary series of paybacks and revenge killings. Kane, along with his brother Les, was one of Melbourne's best-known standover men. He was shot by a lone gunman as he downed a middy. Another suspect, Norman Leung Lee, was shot dead in a bungled $1.25 million robbery at Tullamarine Airport on 28 July 1992.

At Winton in Western Queensland, a prisoner chained to a large log outside marched into the Post Office Hotel – log and all – and ordered a beer. It took three men to wrestle the offender and the log outside. A police station was built soon afterwards

Great publicans

Originally the Anchor and Hope Hotel in Richmond, Victoria was owned by Richmond Football Club legend, Jack 'Skinny' Titus. His mum was well known too, especially for her 'Ma's Sunday Morning Club' a sly-grog shop that she ran at the South Richmond Baby's Health Centre on Sunday mornings. It wasn't the only sly-grog shop in the district. Dickie Riordan used to open his Central Club Hotel in Swan Street on Sunday to cater for thirsty residents.

The Corones Hotel in the south-western Queensland frontier town of Charleville is the stuff legends are made of. Listed by the National Trust, it was built around 1928 on the site of the former Hotel Norman by Harry (Poppa) Corones, a Greek migrant. Corones spent £50,000 on the rambling structure that almost occupies a whole town block. Originally there was a barber shop, a foyer with copper-topped tables and white marble floor, and a dining room. The ballroom was said to have been the finest outside of Brisbane. It also claimed to be the largest hotel outside the capital. The board of Qantas held their first meeting there. Each bedroom opens on to a balcony, while the dining room opens onto a central piazza, which is cool in hot weather.

A legend in the west, Poppa shouted the town of 7000 residents free drinks when he received his MBE in 1965. One story goes that if you don't see him around, the quickest way to find him is to ring up the 'No Charge' key on the cash register in the bar! One time, a race-goer bet 100 bottles of champagne Poppa couldn't serve everyone in the dining room with champers in less than five minutes. A furious flurry of popping cork ensued, and Poppa won the bet. He was licensee of the hotel until 1950, when his son Peter took over.

The one-time publican of the Council Club Hotel in Wangaratta, Victoria had an eye for business. On taking the temperature of his empty bar, he was surprised to find it read 146 degrees Fahrenheit. At the time public servants were allowed to go home if the temperature reached a century, so he casually crossed the road to the court house and showed them the temperature. Soon the courts were empty and his hotel was full!

In early Hobart, the former Phoenix Hotel earned the moniker 'Chopper's' after licensee Chopper Cross. Apparently the nickname, like the licence, was handed down from father to son for generations. The nickname was not entirely inaccurate though because the inn was said to have been one of the basest inns of debauchery in the fledging city, although ironically, Chopper's youngest daughter became a policewoman. The Phoenix was also one of the only places in Hobart in 1855 that you could meet an elephant. Hobart's classy Grand Chancellor (née Sheraton) Hotel was later built on the site of this notorious hotel.

In the early lawless days of Australia, many publicans kept firearms for self-defence. It is not known, however, if this was the case north-east of Brewarrina on the Narran River, NSW, where an eccentric old publican known as Mrs Wilby-Wilby allegedly shot at her customers.

In 1900 gun shearer John Robert (Jacky) Howe, took over the running of the Barcoo Hotel in Blackall, Queensland. Howe set world records for shearing during his career that stood for over 50 years. Howe shore 321 sheep using hand shears and 337 sheep using electric cutters in 7 hours and 20 minutes at Alice Downs in October 1892. The trademark navy blue singlet favoured by workers across Australia was later named after him.

Dubbo historian Bill Hornadge relates a story about an owner of the Macquarie Inn in Dubbo, NSW. George Smith, or 'Dusty Bob' as he was known was once a stock-keeper at Yalcagreen Station. He returned to his hut one evening to see some writing on his door. It posed a problem for him as he couldn't read. Thinking the Crown Lands Commissioner may have passed that way during the day and left an important message for him, he wrenched the door from its hinges and carried it to the nearest settlement several miles away where a settler obligingly deciphered the message: 'Dusty Bob from Yalcagreen, the dirtiest hut keeper ever was seen'.

The Greenock Creek Tavern in South Australia's Barossa Valley was kept by the Schluter family for 106 years from 1870. Perhaps a dynasty of this length inspired a certain Mr Martin. The licensee of the Clarence Hotel in Bellerive, Tasmania, he married the hotel's maid who was 48 years his junior.

The Wallacia Hotel in NSW was the scene of a drama on 24 August 1990 when a live bomb was defused by young Mount Druitt constable Rupert Agnew. The bomb, planted in the cellar of the hotel, was hidden among drums of fuel and petrol-soaked clothes and was set to explode at 1 pm. It was defused at 12.55 pm. That day was the first day on the job for new manager, Mano Gazzoli, who denied having any enemies.

8

Keepers of the peace

Queen of ma heart

Isabel Robinson, 1890s publican of the Royal Mail Hotel, was known as the 'Eulo Queen'. She was described as always 'expensively dressed, her red hair piled high, her blue eyes twinkling and a large area of her creamy bosom visible', and she held court at her bar every night. She was able to handle even the roughest drovers, who used to throw all their pay on the bar and remain drinking to the last penny. Isabel was a champion at billiards and card games and a great favourite of travelling salesmen and overlanders. Although some disgruntled card players whispered that she used a marked deck, they never dared accuse her – the 'Queen' had a fearsome temper and was a brilliant shot.

Breaker Morant (Harry Harbord) was so moved by Isabel's presence that he referred to her in his poem 'West by North again':

The Paroo may be quickly crossed – the Eulo common's bare
And, anyhow, it isn't wise, old man! to dally there.
Alack-a-day! far wiser men than you and I succumb
To a woman's wiles, and potency of Queensland wayside rum.

Way up on the far north coast of NSW, there was a publican known as 'Ma' because she was old enough to be any of her customers' mother, but also because her initials – M.A. (Margaret Alice) – stood proudly outside her pub, the New Brighton at Billinudgel. She started working there in September 1929, and presided over the hotel until her death at 102 on 9 May 1983. Her pub, which was built in 1907 as the Tramway when she was just 26, is now called the Billinudgel Hotel.

In the 1890s the town of Petersburg (now Peterborough) in South Australia was a thirsty town. The barmaid at the Railway Hotel was armed with a tomahawk to chase off drinkers jumping the bar to get to the grog.

Kitty litter

Although never licensed, Kitty Temple's sly-grog shop operated for about 50 years in its Caveton location between Mount Gambier and Nelson. Kitty always had a stock of hard liquor on hand, and was often raided by police, but never caught – she said that she could smell the police from miles away (which wasn't bad, as she kept a herd of goats on the property as well). Kitty inherited the buildings in 1872 after William Temple was fined in 1872 for sly-grogging.

Another woman demanding respect (not to mention equal rights), chained herself to the footrail of the public bar at the Regatta Hotel in suburban Toowong in Brisbane, protesting against the ban on females drinking in public bars.

Collingwood's Grace Darling Hotel and the Sarah Sands Hotel in Brunswick were both named after ships that were named after women. Grace Darling and her father rowed out from the Longstore Lighthouse to rescue survivors of a shipwreck in the early hours of 7 September 1838. The pub was built 16 years after this rescue. Grace died from consumption four years after her heroic deed.

At the Whyte River Hotel near Luina on the rugged west coast of Tasmania in 1914, miners from all around took shelter in the pub as a snowstorm became heavier. They were eventually snowed in, and before long used their supplies of food. The only way through to the nearest town, Waratah, was for the publican's young daughter, Vera Quinton to saddle up her pony for a very cold sixteen kilometre ride. The young heroine had to get her pony unbogged several times and fears were held for her (and consequently for the miners themselves) when she wasn't back by nightfall. But she did get through, supplies arrived and the miners were saved.

> At the Land of Promise Hotel in Hindmarsh, South Australia, a Mr Jarman sold his wife at a well-attended auction, receiving the sum of £1.7.6 from the highest bidder, Charles Goble.

Barmaids

Barmaids are as much a part of the Australian pub as the beer they dispense. However, the authorities haven't always tolerated women trying to make an honest living behind the bar.

Drinkers at Babinda in far north Queensland during the 1910s not only had to contend with a pub run by the government (the State Hotel), with its restricted opening hours, but barmaids were not allowed either. In South Australia before 1908 women could serve behind a bar, but in that year a law was passed preventing all but wives, mothers, daughters, sisters and step-daughters of the publican tending the bar. Others required registration. 401 barmaids were registered in 1909. By 1935 less than 20 remained.

Towards the end of the nineteenth century the barmaids at the Continental Hotel in Melbourne upset the city's traditionalists when they wore bloomers.

At the Globe Hotel in Port Adelaide (now the Golden Port Tavern) in the late 1960s the barmaids wore mini-skirts that were really only long shirts. This change in attire increased the business at the pub from about eighteen kegs per week to about fifty.

'An English barmaid talks'

Licensed Victuallers Gazette, 1930

'It is no longer sufficient for a girl to be pretty and fascinating. This may hold good in certain places with a special clientele, but for the most part capacity as well as good looks is required. No one has a greater need of flattery than the girl behind the bar. All sorts and conditions of men pay her homage. She is, at once, behind the hedge that separates her from the outer world, supremely desirable and quite unattainable. I sometimes think that the ideal barmaid requires as good a brain as a woman in any of the professions. She must learn to judge character quickly, and, above all, must take what is said to her with a grain of salt.'

> Roma's School of Arts Hotel was said to have once housed the town's brothel on its second floor. Trading from 1869 until 1908, the building that was the Bristol and Bath Hotel in Collingwood, Victoria, now houses 'Cromwell Heights', a licensed brothel.

Duels

A romantic legend was born at a Blue Mountains halfway house, Collits Inn at Mount York. Pierce Collits' youngest daughter, Emelia, fell in love with a local bushranger known as Tom. Collits, himself a rogue, enjoyed Tom's company and one night while the two were playing cards in the tap room, Emelia hurried in to warn her lover that soldiers were approaching. Tom hurried away to his hide-out on Mount York.

The redcoats were quartered at the inn and, one of them, Ensign Lake, fell in love with Emelia and asked her to marry him. She refused, but Tom was so unhappy when he heard of the proposal that he sought out the soldier and challenged him to a duel. They fought at the inn and Tom was mortally wounded, dying in Emelia's arms. Emelia refused the renewed advances of Ensign Lake, who shortly afterwards returned to his native England.

Emelia then vowed to marry the first eligible man that entered the tap-room of the inn. This happened to be a 75-year-old widower. When he died two years later, Lake, who was a very persistent wooer, hastened from England to propose again. Emelia once again rejected him and never re-married.

In a more likely version of the story, Emelia fell in love with Lake but her father, being friendly with the local ruffians, forbad her to have anything to do with a redcoat. Emelia swore to marry the next man to enter the inn, who turned out to be 38-year-old John Skeen, a former convict. They were married in Hartley in 1832 and had seven children.

A musical play, *Collits Inn* by T. Stuart Gurr with lyrics and music by Varney Monk, used the hotel as the background for a romantic love story. It was performed at the New Tivoli Theatre in Sydney in 1934, with Marshall Crosby and Gladys Moncrieff in the lead roles of Pierce and 'Mary' (Emelia) Collits.

A duel for a lady's hand was fought at Albury's Globe Hotel, although it was not conventional. This duel was a showdown by champagne. After the 145th round (so they say) the contest was over as one of the protagonists had passed out and was carried off.

One Australian barmaid could very well have become the First Lady of the United States of America. While visiting Kalgoorlie's Hannan's Hotel, Herbert Hoover, the President of the United States between 1929 and 1933, became besotted with the barmaid and was moved to write a poem for her.

Birdwatchers

The demolition of the Surfers Paradise Hotel on Queensland's Gold Coast on 13 September 1983 meant just one thing to many males that had frequented the hotel – the demolition of the 'Birdwatchers Bar'. Built on the busy corner of Cavill Avenue and the Gold Coast Highway, the bar was an institution for unreconstructed males. The blokes would shun the bar, preferring to line up along the glassed windows and watch the girls go by. When the hotel was rebuilt as a multi-storied monolith, the Birdwatchers was kept, but this time using one-way glass.

Another 'Birdwatchers Bar' remains at McGuire's Hotel in Mackay in North Queensland, fronting Wood Street with stools at the best viewing spots.

The Bulli Family Hotel on NSW's south coast hosted infamous crime figure Tilly Devine during the late 1950s. Devine was said to have been involved in protection rackets, sly-grogging and prostitution. But the publican was not too proud to have an association with Devine as she and her party would spend up big in the bar.

Nymphs

The Amber Hotel in Eucla, Western Australia, is one of the most remote hotels in the country but is known to Australians as the home of the 'Nullarbor Nymph'. The story started in the hotel's bar on Christmas Eve 1971, when a journalist overheard a yarn being spun about a girl who 'ran naked with the kangaroos'. The journo commandeered the pub's telex and soon the report was national news. To give credence to the story a picture was required, and a willing model came in the form of the publican's future wife Geniece Scott. Movie and still pictures were beamed to a world-wide audience. The pranksters also encouraged Geniece to run across the Eyre Highway at about the same time as the interstate buses were due.

On the evening of 20 February 1991 a strip act at a gentleman's evening became literally too hot to handle when a fuse box in the front bar of the Brompton Park Hotel in South Australia short-

circuited. The pub was plunged into darkness and flames shot up the wall just as a member of the 'Naked Revue' troupe was about to disrobe. Owner Bobby Russell and a helper extinguished the blaze before the fire brigade turned up.

Opposite the Victorian Trades Hall, the management at the John Curtin Hotel in Carlton instigated controversy in November 1990 when the ACTU black-banned their members from frequenting their 'second Trades Hall' after the hotel employed topless dancers. The union movement decreed that this contravened anti-social and anti-degradation discrimination laws.

Like many pubs in small towns across Australia the River Arms in Ulverstone, Tasmania, is known as the 'Bottom pub'. However this hotel took its name literally and its 'Bottom Bar' was a shrine to buttocks, with pictures of buns plastered all over its walls. The pub even had a yearly contest for the most attractive bum.

John Curtin Hotel, Carlton, Victoria

9

Lawson and Lalor

Henry Lawson liked to drink beer. So much that it became a problem. Money for drink was kept secret from his wife then later not used for alimony payments, which saw him in and out of Darlinghurst Gaol for reneging on maintenance responsibilities. But sadly, if not for the drink, we would never have had Lawson's incisive portraits of turn-of-the-century Australians — the drovers, the shearers and the city-folk — that the more eloquent A.B. Paterson could never quite deliver.

Lawson was born Henry Hertzberg Larsen in a tent on the Grenfell Goldfields on 17 June 1867, the first-born of Peter and Louise Larsen. Although Lawson's parents did not drink, Louisa's father, Henry Albury, ran a shanty on the Eurunderee goldfields, and Peter's father was a heavy drinker who had ended up as a poor potato farmer after once being a pillar of Norwegian society.

Henry had a miserable childhood. His parents bickered, and he was found to be partially deaf at the age of nine. He was a withdrawn child who had to withstand taunts from other schoolchildren and later, after his parents separated and he went to live in Sydney with his mother, from his employers and workmates. It was not until he returned to do some labouring for his father in the Blue Mountains that he felt comfortable in the company of strangers. When his father died, Henry turned to writing after some encouragement from his mother, even though fear of strangers still haunted him.

His first works gave readers of the *Bulletin* a taste of one of his recurring themes, nationalism. 'A Song of the Republic' and 'Hymn of the Socialists' were probably influenced by his work on his mother's *Republican* magazine. However, it was working for his father in the Blue Mountains that introduced him to his favourite subject, the worker.

When he moved back to Sydney, Henry started drinking heavily. His editors at the *Bulletin* suggested he move to Bourke for inspiration and to get away from undesirable influences in Sydney.

He moved into the Central Australian Hotel and painted both that hotel and the historic Carriers Arms. Some of his best writings in this period between 1892 and 1893 were *Tambaroora Jim*, the story of an ordinary bloke but an extraordinary publican, and *Crawalong*. In the poem 'Sweeney', a green city man arrives in a small town called Come-and-have-a-drink (a thinly disguised Bourke) and lectures a drunk. This slice of classic Lawson verse finishes with poignant irony: 'And, perhaps, his face forewarned me of a face that I might see / From a bitter cup reflected in the wretched days to be.'

From 1893 the pub became the setting for some of Lawson's best works. Many had their origins in Bourke, among them four epics. *Send Round the Hat* (1901) chronicled the unusual charity of Giraffe, always on the lookout for an excuse to start up a collection. *The Union Buries its Dead* (1893) tells of a funeral procession watched by curious onlookers from underneath a hotel verandah. 'When the Army prays for Watty' (1893) and *That Pretty Girl in the Army* (1901) tell about the Salvation Army and its relationship to the pubs and drinking men.

Another of Lawson's publican characters was Stiffner. Although inspired by a publican Lawson met when living in New Zealand, there were influences from Bourke and Hungerford in the mean old hotelier as well. Stiffner, named for his previous occupation as a wild dog poisoner, kept the 'Not There' Hotel. He and Poisonous Jimmy in *Poisonous Jimmy Gets Left* (1901) were practitioners of the 'lamber-down' – fawning over their customers while their cheque was still good. They had no patience however, with a broke and drunken shearer. Stiffner and Poisonous Jimmy were fair game for the bush prankster, and in *Taking down Stiffner* and *Poisonous Jimmy Gets Left* Lawson described a series of 'got-at's' between the shanty keepers and their more sober patrons.

Another lamber-down was the publican in the short story *His Brother's Keeper*, who purposely employed pretty barmaids to entice gullible shearers. One pathetic soul fell into the trap, but managed to get his cheque back courtesy of bush parson Peter M'Laughlan, a man respected by everybody except the publican.

Lawson wrote of 'Madam Bong Fong', a brash woman publican talked about around town, but often the first to help out in times of personal crisis; Mrs Spooker in *Table Legs, Wooden Heads* and *Woman's Heart* who had the reputation of being the 'meanest' landlady in the city; and of the 'Pub that lost its Licence' (1911), which was immaculately turned out, but closed by the wowsers of the day.

Lawson theorised about the naming of pubs in *Lord Douglas* (1901), and later vividly described a pro-union pub in Bourke (ironically called the Imperial). He explored the irony of the Shamrock pub run by Jock McPherson and the Robbie Burns, presided over by Pat Ryan in 'The Township' (1919), and bemoaned the beginning of six o'clock closing days in 'In the days when we were Young', one of the last pieces he wrote.

Around the turn of the century Lawson was a member of the infamous 'Dawn and Dusk Club', which coveted beer, cheap wine and conversation. Then it was home to the family on the last tram or ferry.

Lawson frequented many Sydney hotels, including the Ship and Paragon Hotels in Circular Quay, the Marble Bar of Adam's Tattersalls Hotel (now of the Sydney Hilton), and in later years, Dind's Hotel in Milson's Point, which was built in the 1860s and demolished around 1938. Kept by thespian William Dind, it was the type of cosmopolitan gathering place Lawson loved. It was visited infrequently by ferry from Sydney, so extended visits became the norm for Henry. 'Dind's Hotel', written in the year of his death in 1922, documented a prank pulled by men old enough to know better, but young enough to still have the desire for a lark. A horse-borrowing saga ended with the perpetrators joining the victims for a drink afterwards, all finding new soulmates to drink the New Year in. This piece was written a few months before Lawson's death, while he was a patient at the Coast Hospital. It was his last long verse.

Once, during a sobering-up trip with publisher and mentor John Archibald, Lawson insisted on stopping at every pub before they reached the bush. One time Lawson was convinced that he saw a corner pub, and they trotted inside. Archibald was amused when they found that it was a lolly shop, but Lawson was convinced that it had been a pub which had been delicensed.

He was also known to have frequented the Como Hotel in Sydney's South. Lawson wrote brilliantly about the trials of bush publicans. Unlike Stiffner and his lamber-down mob, these were men of good cheer. The bush publican was the first contact for a stranger in a new town, and a sympathetic ear for men with problems. 'The Bush Publican's Lament', 'The Bulletin Hotel' (both 1901) and later the *Unknown God of Narrandera* and *More of the Unknown God*, written after a stint in the 'dry' town of Leeton and frequent visits to 'lawless and godless' Narrandera nearby all feature bush publicans. According to Lawson the bush publican considered it his duty to look after his customers and their finances, even if bankruptcy was either near or upon them.

The *Unknown God of Narrandera* draws comparisons between bush publicans and general storekeepers. The man who runs Buckley's Hotel in Narrandera, puts some bottles on an account for the narrator, never having heard of him but thinking 'it best to take me charnce'. It turns out that he has been a publican for many years, always 'taking his charnce' and living a meagre existence as a result.

Henry Lawson died a poor man on 1 September 1922 at his rented Abbotsford house. The great talent, who in his final years penned lewd and ribald rhymes in bar-rooms for the price of a beer, was honoured by Prime Minister Billy Hughes with a State funeral. He would be pleased to know that at least two hotels have been touched by his work. At Fitzroy North in Victoria, the Circuit Bar was formerly known as the Loaded Dog Hotel after one of Lawson's classic short stories. It came complete with large fibreglass statue of a dog (with blood-shot eyes) enjoying a beer at the bar. There is also a Loaded Dog Hotel in Tarago, NSW.

Eureka

Late one night in early October 1854, drunken diggers Peter Martin and James Scobie chanced upon James Bentley's Eureka Hotel, the most substantial and newest hotel in the Ballarat goldfields. In a short time Bentley had built up quite a reputation but he was selective about who patronised his hotel and he took delight in turning Martin and Scobie away. Scobie in his frustration broke a window. The drunken pair were making their clumsy getaway when they heard voices behind them. They turned around thinking that Bentley was asking them back for a drink, but found a mob almost upon them. They had no time to escape a violent attack with shovels and other implements. Martin was struck down but managed to find his feet and ran. When he returned very shortly, James Scobie was already dead or dying from a blow delivered by Bentley or his cohorts.

This murder triggered events that led to the Eureka Stockade and a defining moment in Australian history. The initial failure of the coroner to disclose the facts of Scobie's death and the delay in bringing Bentley to trial, riled the diggers. There was already disquiet amongst the diggers about the strong-armed methods employed by the police hunting for mining licences. The diggers craved justice and wanted Bentley to face the courts.

Meetings of the diggers followed, and the rabble of men from Ireland, Scotland, England, America and Europe bonded together to protest against the authorities' tactics. A large gathering was held on the morning of 17 October near Bentley's Eureka Hotel, where it was decided a committee should be formed to raise a reward for the prosecution of Bentley. As the day wore on and became warmer, the men became drunk, and a fire broke out in the canvas bowling alley next-door to the Eureka Hotel. It was burnt to the ground amid the cheers of nearly 10,000 diggers.

Victorian Governor Hotham vowed to find a scapegoat, and three men received jail terms. The diggers, by now showing some semblance of unity, and the authorities were heading toward outright conflict. The authorities believed that the miners were ready to attack the camp of the local administration, and sent reinforcements to Ballarat to quell the feared uprising.

The diggers, under the leadership of Irishman Peter Lalor, were actually busy fortifying themselves in a crudely constructed stockade in the Eureka field. They had burned their mining licences in a show of solidarity and were expecting the authorities to undertake a licence hunt. In the early hours of 3 December 1854, choosing the time the diggers would be least prepared, military and police stormed the stockade and woke the weary miners, some only armed with crude implements like picks. Blood flowed, but not much from the soldiers representing the Government of Victoria. In the aftermath of the battle a bounty was put on Lalor's head. He went into hiding at an inn in Meredith, on the Geelong Road, with an injury that meant he subsequently lost an arm.

Diggers and others who had been at the stockade were tried for high treason. Common-sense prevailed however, and they were acquitted.

After the skirmish, in 1855, rebel leader Lalor stayed at Geelong's Young Queen Hotel where a Catholic surgeon removed shrapnel from his arm. It was also in a pub – the Separation Inn near Bannockburn – kept by an Irishman named O'Meara – that Lalor was recognised.

One of two diggers who noticed him was keen to inform the

police at Geelong and collect a reward, but the other was more sympathetic to the Eureka cause. This man, Burns, bought celebration drinks supposedly to toast their newly found wealth, but infact to make his partner fall into a drunken stupor and miss the opportunity to dob Lalor in.

There is now a Eureka Stockade Hotel in Ballarat, although not on the battle-site or the site of Bentley's original pub. It is near to the Stockade, and was originally known as the Australia Felix Hotel when it opened in 1856. There is also a Peter Lalor Hotel, which opened as the Royal Oak Hotel in 1864. This hotel has four murals painted by Ken Palmer on its outside walls depicting scenes of the rebellion.

Soldierly antics

Beer rationing hit hard in far north Queensland during the second world war when soldiers fighting in New Guinea were stationed in the district. As beer glasses were in short supply at the Malanda Hotel, the soldiers fashioned 'Lady Blameys', a bottle of beer with the neck cut off and smoothed over. The rationing meant that the eighteen-gallon keg allowed per day would sometimes be emptied in twelve minutes.

The Barron Valley Hotel in Atherton, Queensland was used as headquarters for General Thomas Blamey and the Australian Officers' Club during the war. In Cairns the Pacific Hotel was also used as an American Red Cross and Australian Army Officers' club.

In 1988 the US Navy voted Rocca's, as the Woolloomoolloo Bay Hotel is commonly known among sailors, the 'best venue in the Pacific'. During the Navy's 75th anniversary in 1988, 17,000 sailors came through the hotel in ten days.

Built originally to serve what was the Northern Territory's most significant aviation centre, the Daly River Hotel was first licensed in 1938 after the town store was established by Bill and Henrietta Pearce in 1930. During the war it was used as a hospital, then as an officer's mess. Near Daly River, the Birdum Hotel was kept busy serving some of the 3000 airmen stationed at what was then the largest airstrip in the southern hemisphere, the Gorrie Airstrip.

The General Gordon Hotel in Homebush, Queensland, is named after Major-General Sir Charles George Gordon, who died in the Sudan War. The Marshall MacMahon Inn at Wallabedah in New South Wales is named after a French Army General, as was Bonaparte's in Brisbane's inner suburb of Spring Hill.

The first licensee of the German Arms Hotel in Hahndorf, South Australia, was Gottfried Lubach, who, as a sergeant at the Battle of Waterloo, sounded the bugle for the Prussian troops on the battleground against the Duke of

Wellington's army. With anti-German hysteria running rife during the first world war, the name of the hotel (and the town) was changed to Ambleside in 1916, but in 1976 it reverted to its original name.

At 10 pm on 31 October 1986 the Hotel Carlton in Brisbane closed its doors for the last time. One of its many fine features was a stag's head, the antlers of which gave the 12 Pointer Bar its name. During the second world war sailors used to toss their caps at the trophy, with drinks shouted for the sailor who managed to hook his hat on one of the antlers.

Relations between American and Australian troops were not always cordial during the war. Some of the most heated clashed in the 'Battles of Brisbane' – between American and Australian troops – took place at the former Gresham Hotel.

At the Continental Hotel in Broome, Western Australia, Air Force pilots were being briefed on their last flight to Perth when the Japanese bombed the Broome airfield in March 1942. On 19 February 1942 the Darwin Hotel was damaged slightly in an air-raid. Some guests left the premises in a hurry, most forgetting to pay their bills. The saloon and public bars are on the site of the former Club Hotel, which fared much worse in the bombing. The Don Hotel also wore the full brunt of the Japanese attack.

Some famous second world war patrons of the Botanical Hotel in South Yarra, Victoria, were officers of the Special Organisations Group. A group of them sailed into Singapore in a *prahu* and sank 48,000 tonnes of Japanese shipping in the harbour.

The Light Brigade Hotel's name is thought to have come directly from the nearby Victoria Barracks. Bendigo's Rifle Brigade Hotel was named after Major Thomas Mitchell's regiment across the road, while Brisbane's LA Hotel used to be known as the Paddo Barracks Hotel, across the road from the Paddington Army Barracks.

10

Wattle it be?

Throughout the history of hotels in Australia, publicans and their customers have come up with many strange phrases. Some may have been imported from England, Scotland, Wales, Ireland, Germany and the many other countries that have contributed to our culture, but others seem uniquely Australian.

Running the cutter

'Running the cutter' was widely heard in the Queensland gold-mining centre of Mount Morgan from the turn of the century to about the time of the first world war.

The 'cutter' is a standard-size billy usually used for brewing tea. Near the end of his shift, the thirsty gold miner would ask one of his juniors to run over to the pub and have the barman fill the billy with beer. Or the cutters would be filled and consumed outside the pub, where the miners could talk, and drink, in relative peace. One small side-street in Mount Morgan was actually known as Cutter Lane, in between the Grand and Imperial Hotels, and was a favourite drinking-spot for the miners.

A variation on 'running the cutter' was when a worker wanted to go straight home but still have a beer after his shift. His wife would ask one of the children to go to the pub and fill the cutter, ready for when dad got home. One miner cut crook once when his boy got thirsty on the way home from the pub and drained half the beer. Topping it up with some river water, he hoped that his father wouldn't notice, but was betrayed by a tadpole.

Ring of beer

This was a game invented by shearers and encouraged by publicans during the cut-out festivities that usually followed the end of a shearing stint. A man who had a cheque to 'knock down' would arrive in the bar and call for a 'ring'. The publican immediately set nine full mugs in a ring on the counter, and the shearer started to work around the ring. After the third mug was empty the publican started re-filling the glasses and then it became a race to see whether the shearer could overtake the publican or vice-versa. The loser had to pay for the beer consumed. With today's beer-dispensing equipment it would be impossible to win the game without updating the rules.

Whenever teamsters and their bullock wagons used to pull up at Ted Connors' Junction Hotel at Bandiana near Wodonga, Victoria, they were greeted with enthusiasm by the local young women. Connors disapproved, and referred to the girls as 'those brazen lumps'. The hotel was then named after the exclamation, but through careless speech, has become known as the Blazing Stump.

Lambing-down

Definitely not in fashion now, but 'lambing-down' was the term used when a publican encouraged the shearers and drovers to 'knock down' their whole pay cheque at the bar. Squatters preferred to pay wages by cheque, avoiding the large cash holdings that attracted bushrangers. The workers went to the pubs to cash their cheques. Most inn-keepers did not hand over cash, but gave the workers credit. They were rarely asked for change. After a customer collapsed in a drunken stupor, the wily publican would drag his body into a empty room and surround him with empty champagne bottles. When the man came to, the publican would tell him that he had shouted champagne for the whole town and that there was no money left in his cheque. Out of the goodness of his heart the publican would allow the unfortunate shearer to stay on for a few days to regain his strength before he returned to work. Sometimes the publican would get the poor fellow to work for him, with harsh labour often the 'sentence', then send him off with rations and a swag in search of more work, knowing that he, or an another like him, would be back at the next shed cut-out.

At the time of the first world war 'lambing down' was becoming less common, but had by no means vanished.

The Australian Hotel at Georgetown, Queensland opened in 1892 and burnt down in 1960. It was rebuilt as the Wenaru Hotel. George Dickenson said that he named it after he became sick of the question: 'When are you going to build that new pub?'

Sign-on Day

Sign-on Day was held in the sugar-cane growing areas of the far north of New South Wales on a Saturday in either May or June. It was the day on which farmers and sugar companies would sign-up cutters for the coming season in a pub. The trade in these hotels on sign-on day was quite unbelievable, especially when the new recruits had to start their demanding work in the fields on the Monday. Sign-off day was even more raucous, with much bantering about the prowess of individual cutting gangs.

The black stump

'Beyond the black stump' is usually a long way away. The myth of exactly where the fabled 'Black Stump' is may be solved by a pub. The Black Stump Hotel at Merriwagga, New South Wales, first licensed to James Nce in 1925, is one of three claimants of the origin of the phrase.

The Black Stump at Coolah, NSW, was a wine shanty. It was closed around the turn of the century, and burnt down in a bushfire in the 1910s and the property on which it stood is still known as the Black Stump.

The Black Stump Hotel at Trunkey Creek is considered the 'Johnny-come-lately' among the contenders. The Atherton Hotel in far north Queensland was known locally as the Black Stump after a fire in 1941 burnt it and an adjacent wooden light pole down. Then a two-storey timber hotel, now a brick hotel, it still carries its nickname.

Some of the variations on the theme include the London Hotel near Ariah Park in NSW's Riverina District, which was also known as the Blazing Stump, as was the hotel of the same name in Wodonga, Victoria. When the Tattersalls Hotel in Bundaberg, Queensland, was destroyed by fire in the 1950s, a temporary bar operated in a shed in the back yard, affectionately known as the 'Charcoal Inn'.

> While the bar sign on the Labour-in-Vain Hotel in Fitzroy depicted a black baby being scrubbed to no avail, the nearby Perseverance Hotel showed the same baby becoming white.

Dog and vomit

Some of the more memorable pub names have included such beauties as the Handy Andy, Jolly Frog Inn, The Man at the Wheel, Shoulder of Mutton, Surely we have done our Duty, Laird O'Cockpen, Frying Pan Inn, Swinging Gate, Catfish, Spotted Cow, Slaughterhouse, Cave of Dunmore, Little House under the Hill, Champion of Freedom, Revolving Battery, Dead Rat, Red Tomato, Doodle Cooma Arms, Who'd-a-thought-it, Industrious Settler, Why Not, What Cheer Inn, Circular Saw, Nil Desperandum Inn, the Goondibluie Greyhound, Mystery Inn and the Errol Flynn in Hobart (where else?).

Also in Hobart at one time were the Brown Bear, Dolphin, Antelope and Woodpecker hotels. Many of these names were copied directly from their British forebears. And continuing in the great tradition of British pub names are such unusual combinations as the Salmon and Ball, Magpie and Stump, Shepherd and his Flock, Dog and Stile, Lamb and Lark, Actress and Bishop, Punch and Bowl, and near Charleville in Queensland, the Dog and Vomit!

Hotels have been named after nearly every trade or occupation, including Hobart's Haberdasher's Arms.

Australian pubs have been named after virtually every major town and county in England, while the Edinburgh Castle, Glasgow Arms, Blue Bell of Scotland, Caledonian, Aberdeen, Commun na Feine and John O'Groats House of Scottish heritage vie with the Erin-go-Bragh, Limerick, Leprechaun, Fermanagh, Harp of Erin, Faugh-a-Ballagh, Armagh, Munster Arms, Ulster, Rock of Cashel, Hibernian and even the Brendan Behan representing the Emerald Isle.

That old standard, the Rose, Shamrock and Thistle, often had its name rearranged in Australia according to the nationality of the publican in charge at the time. There have been three hotels in Australia named after the thirteenth-century Scottish patriot Sir William Wallace, who led a revolt against King Edward I and defeated the English in battle. Wallace was made familiar to Australians as the subject of Mel Gibson's film *Braveheart*.

Other nations have been represented by Goulburn's Bois Chere Hotel and the Espana Hotel (named by the Spanish landlord) at Watsonville in North Queensland. Somewhat predictably, publicans in cosmopolitan Melbourne have come up with the Lantern of Diogenes, Temple of Pomona, Sabloniere, and Piazza Hotels.

The country's indigenous ancestors have not been entirely forgotten, with the Kalkadoon Hotel in Kajabbi, Queensland, which was named to honour the brave Aboriginal warriors who battled the white settlers there.

Cheltenham in Victoria and Scarborough, north of Wollongong, NSW, are two suburbs named after hotels.

Surprisingly, at the time of writing there was only one Kangaroo Hotel, in the old goldrush town of Maldon in Central Victoria, though there are some Wombat Hotels, and pubs named after emus and wallabies.

Adjacent to Boggo Road Gaol, Burke's Hotel in South Brisbane was formerly known as the Red Brick Hotel. The name was taken from the old £10 note, which was known as a brick, because it was predominantly red in colour. Bookies from the race track at the old Gabba course would come into the pub to change their 'red bricks' for smaller notes. It is mere coincidence that the pub was actually a red-brick building.

In 1955 two Melbourne hotels fought for the right to change their names to the Olympic Hotel to cash in on the forthcoming games. The Tanners and Currier's Hotel in Richmond argued it should have the name because of the licensee's Greek heritage. The Albert in Preston said that it was closest to the Olympic Village and should therefore be awarded the name. The Albert won.

Nicknames are an integral part of pub culture in Australia. Often customers are unaware that their watering-hole actually does have an official name. The Wheatsheaf Inn at Beverley, Western Australia, was also officially known as the Settler's Arms and the Beverley Hotel during its fifty-year reign. But all along it was known by the sandal-wood-carters who drank there as the 'Dead Finish'. It was the last pub on their way back from the Swan River and, consequently, the 'dead finish' of their pay.

The West Coast Hotel seems an unlikely name for a pub on Australia's east coast. A local joke goes that the pub was blown over to Cooktown from Western Australia in a tropical cyclone. But the truth is that it was named after goldfields on New Zealand's west coast, from where many of the diggers came.

The other hotel in Cooktown, the Sovereign, became known as the Half Sovereign when a 1959 cyclone blew half of the structure away!

Pure stupidity

Established in 1904 at a cost of £5000 the Esplanade Hotel in Port Hedland, Western Australia, is a two-storey building, a fact that caused no end of embarrassment for owner R.H. McKensie when the hotel was built. No provision had been made for a staircase and the only access to the top floor was a rickety iron staircase attached to an outside wall.

The former Gold Diggers Arms in Lambton, NSW, was the venue for a porridge-eating contest between Lancastrian George Bibby and Scotsman George Penman. Two hundred people in the hotel's long room cheered Bibby on to a mammoth six pints of porridge, while a band played 'Here We Suffer in Grief and Pain'.

In 1907 a stage-coach was held up by bushrangers between Wauchope and Port Macquarie, NSW. The robbers decided to slake their thirst and their free-spending alerted the licensee of the Hastings Hotel, Thomas Grant, to call the police. The fugitives were arrested and the ring-leader served fifteen years, even though the 'weapons' used in the hold-up were made only from wood.

In a well-publicised fracas at the Holiday Inn, Coogee Beach in April 1995, members of AFL team Fitzroy went on a rampage after a loss against the Sydney Swans. The backlash from the incident saw player Jason Baldwin fined and stripped of the club vice-captaincy, and the club doctor was fined $10,000. It seems the Roy Boys make a habit of rampaging. On their end-of-season trip to Bali in 1996, they were kicked out of their hotel after several complaints.

In the last week of 1990 the mascot of the Seven Stars Hotel in Adelaide, 'The Chief', a 1.8 metre high statue of an Indian was stolen. The rare statue was made in the USA and weighed over 110 kilograms. Owner Rob Paech had bought the Indian in a Melbourne shop, and offered a reward of $500 for information leading to its return. It was handed in shortly after.

Licensee David Boyd in 1911 was bottling bulk rum in the sealed-off bar-room of his Bridge Hotel in Nowra, NSW. After finishing his Sunday lunch, he retired to that bar and lit his pipe. He was killed instantly.

Termites eventually destroyed the Wolfram Hotel in Mount Carbine, Queensland, but a disgruntled patron once tried to do the job himself. A crude bomb that he threw at a closed window bounced back and blasted off one of his legs.

A neighbour of the Sportsman's Arms in Broken Hill, NSW kept a rifle trained at the hotel's front parlour. Nobody drank there for fear of being shot, so the story goes.

When John Pascoe Fawkner, publican of the former Fawkner Hotel in Melbourne, returned to Tasmania in 1836 he left George Evans in charge of his pub. Evans in turn transferred it over to George Smith. Upon Fawkner's return Smith refused to give the pub back and a comical battle ensued, with Fawkner's 'troops', armed with cornsheaves from his farm, gradually beating Smith's supporters amid great commotion.

Teacher Mary Molloy ensconced herself during the 1950s in the ruins of the former Globe Hotel in Fowlers Bay, South Australia, and called it her 'castle'. The District Inspector for Education was not impressed, but Mary declined more suitable lodgings.

11
==

Raising a sweat

There has always been some sort of sporting activity going on at every Australian hotel, inn, tavern or bar. It may be no more strenuous than darts or billiards, but could involve the fine arts of pugilism – organised, of course. Many teams were founded in hotels and new sports have been invented there.

Match of the day

The Parade Hotel in East Melbourne, which opened in the 1850s under James Wood, was where Messrs Thompson, Bruce, Wills and Hammersley decided to form the Melbourne Football Club in 1858. The first game of Australian Rules Football was played in Yarra Park opposite the hotel. The hotel later became known as the Melbourne Cricket Ground Hotel (or the MCG Hotel), and many grand football battles have been relived here.

The Collingwood Football Club was founded at the Grace Darling Hotel in Collingwood, where the bar is dedicated to 'those merry souls who achieve contentment before capacity'. In 1855, the Argyle Hotel in Geelong was one of the original headquarters of that city's football club, which played on a paddock adjacent the hotel, the 'Argyle Green'.

Known locally as the 'Boggy Creek Pub', the Sportsman's Arms at Curdie Vale, Victoria, found instant fame as 1989 Brownlow Medallist Paul Couch's local. The celebrations continued for 48 hours non-stop.

Publican Percy Page of the Aberdeen Hotel (now the Circuit Sports Bar) in Fitzroy North, Victoria, devised the system for arranging the Victorian Football League finals series. Not far from there is the Albion Charles Hotel in Northcote, which was known as the Fitzroy Club Hotel in 1992 when the hotel became the team's social club headquarters.

The Junction Hotel, an imposing three-storey, wedge-shaped hotel, was the second hotel in St Kilda. Loyal to the local football team, it flew the St Kilda Football Club flag high when they had a win and at half-mast for a loss. The hotel was opposite the former home-ground of St Kilda, the Junction Oval, but was demolished in 1973 to widen St Kilda Road.

Argyle Hotel, Geelong, Victoria

Football is rarely played in the far north of South Australia at Oodnadatta, and not only because you can skin your knees on the gibber plains. There are scarcely enough men to form a team, and the nearest opposition can be several hundred kilometres away. But in 1922, during the Oodnadatta Cup racing carnival, jockeys and trainers formed a side to take on the locals. The field was marked out, taking up most of the main street, with the goal-posts at one end near the Transcontinental Hotel. At every change, players adjourned to the bar, with the quarter-time breaks becoming longer as the game progressed. Needless to say, the numbers for each team also thinned.

Queensberry rules

There have been many hotels named after the Marquis of Queensberry, and it's only fair that they should be venues where people can enjoy the sport revolutionised by his rules.

At Beechworth's Imperial Hotel in 1874, Ned Kelly fought long-time acquaintance 'Wild' Wright for what was called the 'Unofficial Heavyweight boxing crown of North Eastern Victoria'. Ned won the bout.

While known as the Masonic, Mario's Hotel in Broken Hill was home to the pugilistic arts fraternity in that city, and the Trades Hall Stadium nearby was the sport's main venue. Two famous boxers, Bobby Blay and Fred Henneberry, a former Australian middleweight champ, once lived at the hotel.

Larry Foley, a famous publican of the White Horse Tavern in Sydney's George Street, ran a gymnasium. A boxing trainer, Foley once fought a bout lasting 140 rounds on a hot day that ended in a draw. A rematch was fought in conditions more favourable to his opponent and Foley won in six. Foley was known to many as 'King of the Miller's Point Push'.

There was rivalry in the nineteenth century between the inner Sydney districts of Miller's Point and The Rocks, often resulting in bloody battles between the 'pushes' of each locality. The pubs of the Sydney waterfront were scary places. The larrikin pushes were the forerunners to the bodgies, gangs and posses of later years. The Cabbage Tree Mob were distinctive in their Cabbage Tree hats, Bristley's Mob claimed the Wynyard Barracks area for their own, and the Forties 'smuggled and drank and paid no man reverence'. The Rocks and Miller's Point pushes clashed often, although the Rocks boys, who claimed to have been the original push, were much more powerful.

In the wild and woolly Northern Territory, a small room adjoining the bar at the Tennant Creek Hotel was known as the 'Bull Bar'. It was the scene of many a wrestling-match battle between the larger patrons. Another sport made popular there was 'Bull Fighting', in which men on all fours would snort and bellow until they charged each other in a high-speed head-butt!

Hotels are perfect for pool and snooker competitions. One of the licensees of the Busselton Hotel in Western Australia was Walter Lindrum Snr, whose son spent many hours learning his craft on the billiard tables there. At just 17, he played to hushed audiences at the Katanning Hotel in 1905.

The racing game

Racing journalist Bert Wolfe held a riotous party at Brisbane's Gresham Hotel in 1946. After Bernborough won the T. Ahern Memorial he decreed that celebrations for the superhorse's victory in the forthcoming Doomben Cup should begin 24 hours before the race. The party was one of the most outrageous since the Victory Pacific Bay sortie the year before. Fortunately Bernborough easily won the race. The hotel was well-known amongst the racing fraternity in Brisbane because the T. Ahern Memorial horserace (now the Doomben Hundred Thousand) was named after the second licensee and former BATC Chairman Terry Ahern.

Although it was known locally as Hackett's (the name was painted in huge letters on the roof at one stage), the former Rivette Hotel in Charleville, western Queensland, was named after the first mare ever to win the Caulfield and Melbourne Cups in 1939.

Walter Craig, mine host of Ballarat's famous Craig's Royal Hotel, had a dream in 1870 that his horse Nimblefoot would win that year's Melbourne Cup. Only one thing bothered him – the jockey in his dream was wearing a black armband. Craig died a few days before the horserace and did not live to see Nimblefoot come home with the prize, nor the jockey wearing a black armband. According to another version of the tale, Craig related his dream to his bookmaker, who bet the publican £1000 to eight drinks that the horse wouldn't get home, and that Croydon would fail in the Metropolitan in Sydney. Craig's death meant the cancellation of the bet, but the bookie still paid £500 to Craig's widow to settle when the horse won. In yet another version, bookie Slack wagered £500 to three of Craig's cigars that

Craig's Royal Hotel, Ballarat, Victoria

Nimblefoot would lose. Again, Mrs Craig was said to have benefited from Slack's generosity.

The former Doutta Galla Hotel in Flemington was named from the Aboriginal word 'Dutti Gala' meaning treeless land. Some famous Melbourne Cup winners, including The Barb and Tom Whittler had been stabled there. The pub at the time was known as the Racecourse Inn. Bobby Ramage, the yardman of Footscray's Ship Inn, was jockey of the great racehorse Carbine.

The trainer involved in the 'Fine Cotton' racehorse substitution scandal, Haydn Haitana, was found and captured at the Truro Hotel in South Australia's Barossa Valley. Haitana had substituted a better horse, Bold Personality, for Fine Cotton in order to win a race at Doomben in 1983 in a sting that captured the imagination of the country.

The Early Butcher's Arms in Elizabeth Street, Melbourne, used to advertise that 'gentlemen desirous of trying their terriers will always find a plentiful supply of rats and native cats'.

Chequered flags

A corner of the Adelaide Australian Grand Prix circuit was named after Adelaide's Stag Hotel. Racegoers paid thousands of dollars to watch the action from the hotel's balconies, even between 1992 and 1995 when the hotel was not trading.

The Country Club Hotel in Longford, Tasmania is a two-storey hotel built in 1850 and it was a feature in Longford's two Australian Grand Prix street circuits. During a race in 1963 Lex Davison careered into a pub wall in his 2.7 litre Cooper. Unhurt, he walked straight into the pub for a beer to see out the race on a bar stool. Drivers Bruce McLaren, Jackie Stewart, Graham Hill, Jim Clark, Frank Gardner and Jack Brabham have all raced in Longford. The Country Club Hotel has become partly a racing museum, boasting a Triumph TR 2 raced by Diana Leighton, videos, photographs and posters.

The Anchor and Hope Tavern in Richmond, Victoria, is known for the automobile memorabilia belonging to the former licensee, 'Lead-Foot' Lou Molina. Lou drove in Australian Grands Prix in the 1950s and

won numerous rallies. The pub is a shrine to the automobile, in particular the racing car. All makes and models are represented, even the more exotic marques. Nigel Mansell has been known to pop in, perhaps to have a talk to Lou, whose family still holds an interest in the pub.

At Adelaide's former Circuit Bar, the first in a franchise planned for Australia, sport was the theme, and the main attractions were the sporting memorabilia on display. They included Dick Johnson and Win Percy's Touring Car; an unnamed World Championship 500cc motorbike; an Adelaide 36ers basketball hoop; Collingwood, Hawthorn and Canberra premiership jumpers; Jeff Fenech's and 'Hit Man' Harding's World Championship-winning gloves; a Centenary Test cricket bat; Craig McDermott's cricket shirt; and various bent fuselage of Formula 1 Grand Prix cars. Another feature was the 'Circuit Wall of Wank', an autograph board of the stars.

The Royal Hotel in the Townsville suburb of West End was once a venue for cock-fighting.

On the water

The Seacliff Hotel in Adelaide uses a boat built by Sir James Hardy when he was just 14 as a salad bar. In early days Australia's first rowing headquarters were at Sydney's Scullers Hotel. Edward Trickett, the first Australian to win the World Sculling Championships – in 1876 on the River Thames – was the proprietor of the Oxford Hotel in Rockhampton, Queensland.

Close to the Yarra River, Richmond's Prince Alfred Hotel is home to Melbourne's rowing fraternity. It is decorated with Kings Cup-winning boats and photographs of famous patrons including dual Olympic Gold medallists, the 'Oarsome Foursome'.

The City Rowers' Tavern in Brisbane opened in late 1989 as a theme tavern, the theme being the old boys' rowing clubs and the 'old school tie'. One feature is the honour board listing winners of Head-of-the-River regattas from 1908.

Further north, the Gregory Downs Hotel in north-western Queensland is famous for its 42-kilometre down-the-river canoe race. The pub was originally a shanty across the river from a cattle station. It was found that the cattle business and the hotel did not mix, so the homestead was moved to the western side of the Gregory River.

Balmain's Riverview Hotel was once owned by Dawn Fraser, swimming legend and former member of the NSW parliament, who was raised in the suburb.

The former Grand Natatorium Hotel in Chippendale housed a swimming pool in the basement. The NSW Amateur Swimming Association was established there.

The NSW Surf Life Saving Association had their first meeting in the Light Brigade Hotel at Woollahra in Sydney's eastern suburbs around the turn of the century.

On offer at the Orrong Hotel in Armadale, Victoria, in the late nineteenth century was a greasy pole, and sometimes, a greasy pig. Once, a pig escaped, sped out the door, then disappeared in the nearby mud.

In the slips

The Three Tuns Hotel, opened by Richard Driver in 1823 on the corner of Elizabeth and King Streets in Sydney, was one of the birthplaces of Australian cricket.

The Malanda Hotel in far-northern Queensland hosted famous NSW cricketers – including Bradman, Benaud, Morris, McCabe, Oldfield, Kippax, Jackson and Davidson – when they were in town guesting for Jack Chegwyn's eleven.

Australian cricket captain Warwick Armstrong bet he could hit the ball into the Star Hotel at Walhalla, Victoria, during an exhibition match at the nearby oval but instead he holed out to a Mr Merrington on the boundary. Merrington was very keen to play that day, having walked from his home in Aberfeldy to Walhalla and back, a distance of 90 kilometres.

The Leg Trap Hotel, West Lakes, SA, derived its name from two of its three owners, Australian Test captains Ian and Greg Chappell.

🍺 The Caxton Hotel in Brisbane's Petrie Terrace tirelessly promotes the sport of marbles. Since 1983 the hotel has hosted the marbles world championship, which also features a parade of competitors down Caxton Street. The proceeds of the well-attended event are donated to the Children's Hospital.

Hoofing it

The first meeting place of the Stawell Athletic Club was held at the Star Hotel on 14 January 1878, when they adopted the rules from the Ararat Club as their own. This club grew to host the Stawell Gift, the richest professional footrace in the world, held every Easter. The pub closed in 1916.

The cinder track at Botany's Sir Joseph Banks Hotel hosted the Botany Harriers, formed there in 1907. The owner in 1884, Frank Smith, promoted the footrace known as the St Patrick's Day Handicap. The present building was constructed in 1926.

The walls of the City to Surf Bar of the Bondi Regis Hotel are adorned by memorabilia of starts and finishes of the famous footrace. Built in 1920 at a cost of £17,000, the pub was lauded eight years later as the 'Finest Seaside Hotel in Australia'.

🍺 In 1989 the Sedan Hotel in South Australia was the venue for the Australian Marbles Championships, brainchild of hosts 'Wild Bill' Laws and his wife 'Dizzy' Dawn.

Lucky strikes

At the rear of the Goldfields Hotel was the Northern Territory's first casino, albeit an illegal one. It was run by Cannon Lloyd, an expatriate Queenslander, in a long iron shed with benches and a dirt floor. The tables were always full despite the basic decor. A bet was two-bob minimum, but could be as high as £10,000.

When the Boolaroo Hotel in New South Wales, formerly known as the Sulphide Hotel, was condemned and torn down in 1968 it revealed hidden treasure – £2500 worth of coins underneath the building which had slipped through the floorboards of the two-storey weatherboard pub.

The Wrest Point Casino in Sandy Bay opened in 1973 as Australia's first legal casino. The opening of the complex had a dramatic effect on Tasmania's tourist numbers, which rose 40 per cent on the previous year.

The Eldo Hotel (named after the European Launcher Development Organisation) in the northern South Australian town of Woomera was the first venue in the state (outside the Adelaide Casino) to install coin-operated gaming machines. As the hotel is situated on Commonwealth land, the embargo put on the starting date for pokies in other South Australian hotels did not apply. Poker machines were legal in South Australia's pubs from 25 July 1994. The machines in Woomera were launched with a rocket countdown on 25 March 1993.

Although some pubs have luck on their side, some choose not to push it. The School of Arts Hotel in Roma, Queensland, was said to close when twelve kegs had been consumed in one day, as to end on thirteen was unlucky.

Room 13 of the Palace Hotel in Southern Cross, Western Australia, may or may not have proved unlucky for the guests within, as it was the one used by the town's drunks to sleep off their hangovers.

Michael Ryan took no chances with his Irish Harp Inn in Bankstown, NSW. The pub was to be built on the hanging site of two bushrangers. Ryan removed all the soil from that spot in order to stave off bad luck.

12

Welcome to the wrecking-ball

Even though the recorded history of our country is comparatively short, giant chunks of our heritage have already disappeared in clouds of brickdust and tears. Pubs have not been spared; many have crumbled before developers' wrecking-balls. Here follow the stories of some of the most heart-wrenching demolitions.

The Bellevue

Opening in 1859 as a boarding house for young ladies, then converted to a private hotel two years later, the Bellevue Hotel first traded under the name of Zahel's in 1875. In 1886 it became the Bellevue Hotel and stood proudly on the corner of George and Alice Streets, Brisbane, for 93 years. Built to complement Parliament House opposite, the hotel was to be the largest and most completely furnished and fitted hotel in the colony.

Cast iron was used liberally on the balustrades of the two balconies and the wide, shady verandahs were designed to keep out the hot Brisbane sun. The Bellevue became a Brisbane landmark that hosted dignitaries such as The Queen Mother, Princess Alexandra, Sir Robert Menzies and stars of stage and screen Frank Sinatra, Marlene Dietrich, Vivian Leigh and Katherine Hepburn. The hotel was in a quiet corner of town and the rise of motel accomodation in the 50s and 60s had a severe effect on inner-city hotel accomodation. Alas, in 1967 the Bellevue was bought by the Queensland Government to accomodate country parliamentarians and for use as a store-room. Many lobbied against the hotel's closure, among them the pastoralists who had frequented the hotel (and helped keep the government in power), architects and bodies such as the Conservation Council.

The hotel ceased trading on 31 December 1970, and was used by the Queensland government until 1973. In November of that year the destruction began. Surrounding trees were lopped, and seven months later the decorative cast-iron lacework was stripped. The once-proud hotel was further demeaned when the verandah and balconies were removed in early 1979.

On Saturday 21 April 1979, the first trench-digger arrived to start the demolition of the National Trust-listed hotel. People had battled to save it for nine years but to no avail. It was pulled down amid the din of protesters' car-horns.

Since then Brisbane has lost more of its fine old hotels, the Carlton and New York, both demolished in the REMM–Myer retail development, and Her Majesty's among them. Some classic pubs remain – we can only hope that the Empire and Royal George Hotels in Fortitude Valley, and the city's Port Office and Transcontinental, will stay intact for our grandchildren to enjoy the hospitality those hotels have offered for generations.

In 1973 Buchanan's Hotel, built in 1902 for David Buchanan, featured in an Australian stamp series depicting beautiful buildings. It was in very good company – the Sydney Opera House, Como House in Melbourne, and St James Church in Sydney were also featured.

The former Royal Hotel in Sydney was the first hotel in Australia to have been built with the aid of an architect's plans. The architect was John Verge and he went on to become one of the greatest names in Australian architecture of that period. The original Royal burnt down on 17 March 1840, a loss said to have been worth £12,000.

The Menzies

Gold fever bought Archibald Menzies and his wife, Catherine, to Melbourne from Liverpool in 1852. The Menzies Private Family Hotel on LaTrobe Street was built on land reputedly bought from Governor Charles LaTrobe. Diggers who made good were the original mainstay of the business, but it quickly grew to become one of the city's finest hotels, frequented by the squattocracy.

Menzies, flush with the success of his hotel and buoyed by a substantial gold-mine investment, commissioned architect Joseph Reed to draw up plans for a large hotel on the corner of Bourke and William Streets. Built at a cost of £31,000, the three-storey Menzies Hotel had 48 rooms for accommodation, large public areas, billiard rooms and cosy private bars when it opened on 11 November 1867. The hotel's spectacular Winter Garden, designed by artist Phillip Goatcher, came complete with tropical decor and a huge stained-glass ceiling. Goatcher's commission was then extended to include the main hall and music rooms.

Federal Hotels bought the Menzies Hotel in 1936. Early in 1967 they put it up for sale. The hotel was a going concern, but the potential for multi-storied development on the site was enormous. 'Big Australian' BHP bought the property with the intention of demolishing the old hotel and building its new head office. Early the next year a giant auction was held, and the original fixtures, ornaments, furniture and stock sold in just seven days. The walls came down later in 1969.

For 100 years, the Menzies Hotel commanded a special place in the hearts of Victorians. It had put up such luminaries as Anthony Trollope, J. Edgar Hoover, C.J. Dennis, Alexander Graham Bell, Danny Kaye, Yehudi Menuhin, Mark Twain and countless royals and heads of state (it was the first hotel in Australia to accomodate royalty). Within its walls General Douglas MacArthur had commanded the South and Western Pacific operations during the second world war and Dame Nellie Melba had complained 'I hate this bloody pub,' even though her father had built the hotel years before and it was the venue for one of her triumphant comebacks.

The National Trust-classified Sea Horse Inn at Boydtown, NSW, was built in 1843, when Ben Boyd dreamed of creating a major town in Twofold Bay on the NSW south coast. An Elizabethan-style hotel that reflects the grandeur of Boyd's plans, it is the only building (with the exception of Boyd's Church) still standing representing Boyd's vision to create a city to rival that of Sydney.

Originally built to become the summer residence of the Western Australian Governor, the building that became the Majestic Hotel in the Perth suburb of Applecross was never used for that purpose. It is said that the governor was initially pleased when he inspected the building, but when he came to the bathroom, he was less than impressed, and described it as 'unfit for human habitation'. The builder was a land-developer who thought that it would be prestigious to have the Governor living in their suburb. A block of flats now occupies the site.

The previous summer residence of the Governor of Western Australia was built on Rottnest Island in 1864. It later became the Rottnest Hotel, or, unofficially, the 'Quokka Arms'.

The South Australian

There were tears all round in the state of South Australia when the 'South' finally fell. It had been opened in 1879 by Henry Trew and was then known as the South Australian Club Hotel. Adjacent to the rail terminus, the South became the haunt of the wealthy squattocracy, at the same time nurturing a growing reputation as a family hotel. The polished floors and walls of the Military Officers' Club on the first floor contributed to the exclusive atmosphere.

Twenty years later a new three-storey façade was added to the building, by now known as the South Australian, and extra bedrooms were added to bring the total number up to one hundred.

Although immensely popular in the early 1900s the South seemed to come into its own later in the twentieth century. The hotel's celebrations for VE day in 1945 were the biggest in Adelaide, and when Japan surrendered the South held 'the greatest and brightest celebration for many years', according to the Adelaide *Advertiser*.

Beatlemania consumed Adelaide in 1964 when Liverpool's Fab Four visited (although three because Ringo Starr was ill and did not tour). Pandemonium took over when the Beatles greeted a teeming throng of fans from the hotel's balcony. Adelaide turned out the largest reception the band had encountered anywhere.

Regardless of its popularity, real estate barons deemed that the piece of land on which the South stood was far too valuable to be taken up by a hotel of comparatively small size. The writing was on the wall when the Head Waiter of fifty years, Lewy Cotton, left on 31 December 1970. Five months later the rumour was confirmed. The 'Stop Press' column in the *Advertiser* simply stated 'The South is Sold', and soon afterward the Ansett Transport Group unveiled plans for a multi-storied international standard hotel. A month-long wake for the old pub followed, and an auction of goods and chattels was hugely popular. The hotel was delicensed on 26 June 1971, and in October a fire broke out and reduced the deserted hotel to a shell.

In the years since the site has had its fair share of operators. The nondescript Ansett Gateway Inn replaced the South, but its spirit was lost.

Later, in the 1980s, it was developed into a true international standard hotel when it became the Terrace Hotel. In the 1990s, the Intercontinental Hotel chain took over, becoming the second hotel in that chain operating in Australia. In the 1990s it has been managed by the Stamford Group, the name changing to the Stamford Plaza Hotel.

It has taken nearly thirty years for some of the South's old patrons to return to the site.

The Aurora

The hotel that stood on the south-eastern corner of Adelaide's Hindmarsh Square was known as the Black Eagle in 1859, then the Marquis of Lorne and the Marquis of Queensberry. It became best known as the Aurora before it closed on 23 October 1983. The Baulderstone Group bought it and it was destined to become a pile of rubble before rising phoenix-like as a six-storey office complex.

A picket-line gathered around the hotel when its fate became known, and the Aurora Heritage Faction was born. Although the group failed in its attempt to save the hotel, it became notorious for its militant and physical protests.

Aurora Hotel, Adelaide

The Labor premier at the time, John Bannon, claimed that the Aurora Hotel did not appear on any heritage lists and columnist Max Harris once described the old hotel as a 'comic eyesore'. He said that a nearby tin shed had better claims to preservation. In the face of this opposition not even the chairman of the South Australian History trust, Norman Hetherington, who delivered a eulogy in front of the hotel dressed in a dinner suit, could save the hotel. The demolition started in the early hours of 3 December 1983. No attempt was made to salvage any of the iron lacework, timber joinery or glass, as they were crushed under MacMahon's bulldozers. There were no souvenirs.

The Aurora Heritage Faction met for the last time in August, 1995. According to the group's last chairman, Andrew Cawthorne (who was in the first picket-line twelve years earlier), the group had achieved just what it intended – 'to make preservation of our heritage a bread and butter planning issue, not just the domain of hairy left-wingers'. Over the years the AHF had support from all sectors of the community – members of parliament rubbed shoulders with university professors, lawyers, the unemployed and tradespeople.

Although it was built at a cost of $300 million using architectural styles spanning two centuries, the Le Meridian Hotel in Melbourne (formerly the Menzies-at-Rialto) caught the interest of heritage groups because of its toilets. Hidden at the rear of the original Rialto building were five antique toilets, which were shown on the original Rialto plans in 1890. The Historic Buildings Council argued that the lavatories were historically important, having been there before the city had its first sewerage system, and it was deemed that they be saved from demolition.

Petty's

Originally the manse of controversial clergyman and politician Dr John Dunmorme Lang and popular with new immigrants, the Cummings Hotel was built for William Cummings in 1828 on a site upon Church Hill that Governor Phillip coveted for the nation's first Government House. Cummings, who claimed that he had affidavits from the leading medical men in Sydney testifying that it was the healthiest site in the city, stayed only three years, leaving to take over the Ship Inn at Liverpool. The new owner, Thomas Petty, took over in 1836, and, although he was the licensee until he died ten years later, the hotel kept his name until it closed in 1950.

Under the watchful eye of publican John Williams, Petty's Hotel became the nation's premier hotel, at least until the Menzies in Melbourne was built. Fine food and good service were always offered at the tastefully furnished hotel. Petty's popularity led to regular extensions, unfortunately, the last in 1939 when new bars were built in what had been Mrs Lang's sitting room.

It was a sad day for many in Sydney when the management closed the bar-room for the last time in 1950. The building was used again, from 1952 as the headquarters of the Australian Red Cross blood service, but was demolished in 1975.

Another hotel to be sacrificed in the name of progress was the Palace in Perth. It stood on the site of perhaps the first hotel in Western Australia, the George IV Hotel, opened in 1830 by William Dixon. After a succession of name-changes – the King's Head, Leeder's and the Freemasons – it became the Palace in 1895 when John deBaun commissioned architects Porter and Thomas to build a hotel befitting what he thought would become a grand city.

A three-storey pub of impressive dimensions on a prominent city corner, the Palace represented gold-boom grandeur, with its cedar structures, marble fireplaces and moulded ceilings. It later gave its name (and its life) to a 48-storey Bond Corporation edifice known as Palace Tower.

The unauthorised demolition of Perth's heritage-listed Railway Hotel over the weekend of 4–5 July 1992 sparked a row in which heritage minister, Jim McGinty, said he would seek an order directing those responsible to rebuild the historic hotel. The façade of the hotel was rebuilt but the building no longer serves its original purpose.

Hope for the future?

One example of heritage preservation exists at the Port Arthur Historic Site in Tasmania. The Hotel Arthur was licensed in 1921, and was housed in a building built around 1847 as the lodgings for Deputy Commissary-General Thomas Lempriere. The following year it became the penal colony's medical officer's house, then later the schoolmaster's residence in the 1870s. After the penal colony closed in 1877, the house was bought by a surveyor, and then used as a guest house named Tasman Villa.

The hotel was delicensed in 1959 when the government took over the site to develop the historical site, and all 'post-convict-era' additions were demolished.

The Sydney Hilton offers another good-news story. George Adams, who arrived in Australia in 1855, borrowed money to buy O'Brien's Hotel in Sydney in 1878. In order to pay off the debt he started a small lottery offering £900 first prize on the running of the

Sydney Cup. This system became very lucrative, but in the end was banned in NSW and Queensland.

Adams was able to pay back his debts and, in the face of competition, commissioned architect Varney Parkes to build the most elaborate hotel in Sydney. Opening in 1893, the hotel was known as the Tattersalls. It cost £22,000 and featured works of marble, mirrors, beautifully turned wood, paintings and stained glass. The hotel was illuminated by powerful light from glittering chandeliers and was described as having the 'handsomest marble hall in Australia, worthy of London or Paris'. The Tattersalls was demolished in 1969 to make way for the present Sydney Hilton, but the magnificent marble bar from the old pub was meticulously saved and installed in the new Hilton. The Marble Bar, as it is now, is true to Adams's ambition – the most beautiful bar in the country, perhaps the world.

At around 8 metres by 5 metres and with a bar measuring 2 metres by 3 metres, the Dolly Pot Inn in Tennant Creek in the Northern Territory was hailed in 1935 as the smallest pub in Australia. Unable to cater for a mob with a big thirst, patrons used to congregate near the back door of the inn and lob their empties into a heap at the rear of the pub.

When the town had outgrown the tiny inn, so too had the pile of bottles out the back. Although the white ants have taken over the building, the pile of bottles stood for a long time afterwards. Original owner Harold Nelson's son, Jock, later went on to become the Territory's first Member of the House of Representatives and then later the Territory's Administrator.

Dubbed the world's first international-standard dug-out hotel, the Desert Cave Hotel at Coober Pedy in the north of South Australia opened for business in April 1987. Like the majority of Coober Pedy's housing it was built underground to take advantage of the cool temperature of the earth. Dreamed of by the late Umberto Coro, his son Robert turned the vision into reality when work commenced in 1984.

Pubs are usually associated with a different type of spirit, but it is no wonder that they are often said to be haunted. Where else would you like to spend eternity?

On 22 October 1892, Lucretia Dunkley, the licensee of the former Three Leg O'Man Hotel, was hanged after being found guilty of murdering a wealthy pastoralist and looting his body of 500 sovereigns. After the hanging Dunkley was decapatated for medical examination. Her headless body haunted the pine trees in front of the gaol, the most recent sighting being in Easter 1961 when two campers heard sobbing near the ruins of Dunkley's hotel. They went to investigate and were confronted by the headless Lucretia moving amid the ruins of her pub.

The Peninsula Hotel in Mandurah, Western Australia, used to be haunted but since the hotel itself won a reprieve from execution in 1986 the ghost has not been seen. It may have been the ghost of former publican William Brown, who was found floating in a creek near the hotel with fatal stab wounds to his face and neck.

Both of the old hotels at Port Arthur, Tasmania, the Arthur and the Carnarvon, were said to have been haunted, and is that any wonder given the settlement's rugged convict history? It's a surprise that any self-respecting ghost would wish to return.

Smacking of a conspiracy between coach-drivers and publicans, a spectral figure would appear at midnight every night between Wanganella and Pine Ridge in New South Wales on the coach's regular route. The ghost was seen carrying its own head and riding a snow-white cobby horse. Relieved passengers would shout the driver and the crews of the coaches at least one round once they had reached the pub safely. Accounts of the ghost varied among the coach-drivers, although all claimed they had seen him.

The title of Australia's most haunted hotel is claimed by the Coach and Horses Hotel, previously the Clarkefield in Clarkefield, Victoria. Built in 1857 as a Cobb and Co. staging post, locals have numerous stories about things that go crash in the night there. An eyewitness, Margaret Hunter, claimed to have felt an 'unearthly chill' just before a water jug from the other side of the room levitated and then dropped, smashing on the floor. Licensee Steve Dudley said, 'Our agreement is to work here for twelve months – and we won't let the ghost beat us. But this is the worst time my wife Debbie or I have ever experienced.'

Perhaps more guilt than ghoul inspired the ghost story at the Wiseman's Inn, in New South Wales. This hotel is said to have been haunted by the ghost of Jane, the first wife of original licensee Solomon Wiseman. She fell over, or was thrown over, the upper balcony on to the steps below in 1820. They say that her blood can be seen on the white steps on moonlit nights. The Sydney *Gazette* of 28 July 1821 reported that she 'died on Friday last after a long bout with a lingering illness'.

Unexplained supernatural happenings occur near where the Min Min Hotel was burnt to the ground in the early part of this century. This area of Western Queensland is supposedly the home of the mysterious Min Min light, which has featured in legend and verse and has been seen by people for nearly a century. Said to resemble a car headlight, the Min Min is sometimes stationary, sometimes on the move, sometimes even following or chasing the witnesses. Science is at a loss to explain the mysterious light, but some of the theories include a giant swarm of fireflies, or an owl that has brushed against some unknown luminous substance.

Hotel staff say the Fountain Inn in Parkside, South Australia is haunted by Jack, the spirit of a fireman who died on the premises fighting a blaze years ago. They leave glasses of beer for him in the front bar each night.

One of the newest ghosts resides at the Hub Tavern at Aberfoyle Park in South Australia. The unknown guest, which will only make its presence felt at night, fiddles with the electrical fittings and appliances.

Publican Edward Cullen hung himself in the Bulli Family Hotel in 1930 after an altercation with his wife. She remarried and her new husband became the licensee. Cullen's ghost still haunts the hotel, with one publican swearing that the locked bathroom – the room in which Cullen died – has been found unlocked in the morning on many occasions.

The ghost of an old Aboriginal lady appears at the Corio Hotel in Goolwa, South Australia, once or twice a year. And the Watheroo Station Tavern at Watheroo, Western Australia has a ghost of a young lady who wanders through the kitchen on occasions.

The Leap Hotel overlooks Mount Mandarana or the Leap in Queensland, where an Aboriginal woman is said to have thrown herself off the peak to avoid being captured by white men.

Perhaps the most poignant haunting is that of the Quindanning Tavern, Western Australia. The ghost of a four-year-old girl, who drowned in a dam, sometimes joins the late-night drinkers.

Author's note

This book could not have been compiled without the generous assistance of many people. The complete list is much too long to document, but I thank everyone who has given me help, and apologise for not mentioning you all personally.

Special thanks to Ian Horne and all at the Australian Hotels Association of SA; Richard Mulcahy AHA National Executive; Don Taggart of the St Kilda Historical Society; the Bray Reference Library, Adelaide; Mitchell Library, Sydney; LaTrobe Library, Melbourne; Oxley Library, Brisbane; Tasmaniana Library, Hobart; Angela Kearney AHA Tasmania; Gavin Joel and Kathryn Blake AHA Victoria; Betty Malone of the Prahran Historical Society; Michael Firkins and Lyppard SA; Cheryl Heritage, Brewarrina, NSW; Marius Webb; the late Clifton Pugh.

Thanks to the various local governments, shires, and city councils around the country that assisted me, and especially to the librarians. Many thanks indeed to the historical societies and museums around the country. You do a fantastic job in keeping the spirit of Australia alive.

Also thanks to Ann Moody, Great Lakes Hotel, Miena, Tas; Anne Beggs Sunter, Buninyong, Vic; Australian Council of National Trusts; Carlton and United Breweries (Qld); Cascade Brewing Company, Hobart; Cliff Halsall, Euroa, Vic; Commissioner of Licensing, Tasmania; Darwin Hotel, Darwin; Devonport Promotions and Development Authority; Don and Lesley Graham, Bellevue Hotel, Newcastle; the late Don Dunstan, Norwood, SA; the late Fred Daly, Canberra; Gillian O'Hara, Katanning, WA; Gordon Clarke, Tullah, Tas; John Cook and Norma Wynd, Camperdown, Vic; History Trust of SA; Jean Carmody, Cudgewa, Vic; John Conry and the NSW AHA; Joyce Beikoff, Walkerston, Qld; Kath & Allen Hanson, Bush Inn, New Norfolk, Tas; Linda Rainsford, German Arms, Hahndorf, SA; Liquor Administration Board, NSW; Liquor Licensing Commission, Vic; Lovann Johns, Country Club Hotel, Yea, Vic; Melinda Wakeman and the AHA of WA; Michael Hudson and the QHA; Mick Roberts, Bulli, NSW; National Trusts of NSW and Queensland; Northern Territory Archives Service; Northern Territory Tourist Commission; QHA Central Division; Queensland Dept of Tourism, Sport and Racing; Ranges Hotel, Gembrook, Vic; Ross Wark, Newcastle, NSW; Swan Breweries; Tammi Potter, Watheroo Station Tavern, Watheroo, WA; the late Peter Brien, Alberton, SA; Tooth Breweries (NSW); Jo Tidy, Parmelia Hilton, Perth; Corones Hotel, Charleville; Sydney Hilton; Melbourne Hilton on the Park; Hero of Waterloo Hotel, Sydney; Hope and Anchor Tavern, Hobart; the Ettamogah Pub, Table Top, NSW; the Pub with no Beer, Taylors Arm, NSW; Walkabout Hotel, Nhulunbuy and the Tullamore Hotel, Tullamore, NSW.

For comments, complaints or contributions contact me at spiky@senet.com.au.

Sources

Atherton Centenary Committee, *Tall timber and golden grain; Atherton 1885–1985*, Atherton, Qld, 1985

Bacon, Richard, and Woodberry, Joan *Battery Point (Tasmania) sketchbook*, Rigby, Adelaide, 1978

Baglin, Douglass, and Austin, Yvonne, *Waterholes of Western Australia*, Murray Child, French's Forest, NSW, 1979

Baglin, Douglass, and Austin, Yvonne, *Australian pub crawl*, PR Books, French's Forest, NSW, 1989

Bain, Mary Albertus, *Ancient landmarks: a social and economic history of the Victoria district of Western Australia*, University of Western Australia Press, Nedlands, WA, 1975

Barker, Anthony J., and Laurie, Maxine, *Excellent connections: a history of Bunbury, Western Australia, 1836–1990*, City of Bunbury, Bunbury, WA, 1992

Bayley, William A., *Behind Broulee: History of Eurobodalla Shire, central south coast, New South Wales*, Eurobodalla Shire Council, Moruya, NSW, 1978

Blanks, Harvey, *A story of Yea: the 150 year history of the shire*, Hawthorn Press, Melbourne, 1973

Bradfield, Raymond A., *Castlemaine, a golden harvest*, Lowden Publishing Co., Kilmore, Vic, 1972

Brodsky, Isadore, *Sydney's little world of Woolloomooloo*, Old Sydney Free Press, Neutral Bay, Sydney, 1966

Bushby, John E.P., *Saltbush country: History of the Deniliquin district*, John E.P. Bushby, Deniliquin, NSW, 1980

Butel, Elizabeth, *Kings Cross album: pictorial memories of Kings Cross*, Atrand Pty Ltd, Darlinghurst, Woolloomooloo & Rushcutters Bay, Sydney, 1984

Carroll, Brian, *An illustrated history*, City of Preston, Preston, Vic, 1985

City of Richmond, *Copping it sweet: Shared memories of Richmond*, City of Richmond, Carringbush Regional Library, Melbourne, 1988

Coleman, Dudley, 'Golden heritage: A story of Renmark', *Advertiser*, Adelaide, 1954

Cooper, John Butler, *The history of St Kilda: From its first settlement to a city and after, 1840 to 1930*, Printers Proprietary Limited, Melbourne, 1931

Cross, R.L., *Bygone Queanbeyan*, Queanbeyan Publishing Co., Queanbeyan, NSW, 1985

Cusack, Frank, *Bendigo: A history*, Heinemann (Australia), Melbourne, 1973

Davidson, Bonnie, *Called to the bar: 150 years of pubs in Balmain & Rozelle*, Balmain Association, Balmain, NSW, 1991

Dormer, Marion, *Settlers on the Marthaguy in Western New South Wales*, Macquarie Publications, Dubbo, NSW, 1979

Dunlop, E.W., *Harvest of the years: The story of Burwood, 1794–1974*, Council of the Municipality of Burwood, Burwood, NSW, 1974

Dunstan, Arthur, *Publicans and sinners*, Rigby, Floreat Park, WA, 1986

Elliott, John, *Southport-Surfers Paradise: An illustrated history*, Gold Coast and Hinterland Historical Society, Southport, Qld, 1980

Farwell, George, *Ghost towns of Australia*, Rigby, Adelaide, 1975

Farwell, George, *Requiem for Woolloomooloo*, Hodder and Stoughton, Sydney, 1971

Footscray City Council, *Footscray's first 100 years: The story of a great Australian city*, The *Advertiser* in association with Footscray City Council, Footscray, Vic, 1960

Freeland, J.M., *The Australian pub*, Sun Books, South Melbourne, Vic, 1977

Gibbney, H.J., *Canberra 1913–1953*, Australian Government Publishing Service, Canberra, 1988

Gerritsen, John, *Tibooburra – Corner country*, Tibooburra Press, Tibooburra, 1981

Gibson-Wilde, Dorothy, *A pattern of pubs: Hotels of Townsville 1864–1914*, History Dept, James Cook University, Townsville, Qld, 1988

Gliddon, Joshua Wickett, *Phillip Island in picture and story*, Committee of Trust 'Warley' Bush Nursing Hospital, Phillip Island, 1958

Godfrey, Margery, *Waratah – pioneer of the West*, Municipality of Waratah in association with Morvale Investments, Waratah, Tas, 1984

Hammond, Joyce, *Bridging the gap: Shire of Goulburn 1871–1971*, Council of the Shire of Goulburn, Nagambie, Vic, 1971

Harvey, Anthony, *The Melbourne book*, Hutchinson of Australia, Richmond, Vic, 1982

Hewat, Tim, *Bridge over troubled waters: A history of the Shire of Strathfieldsaye*, Macmillan, South Melbourne, 1983

Hoad, J.L., *Hotels and publicans in South Australia 1836–1984*, Gould Books, Adelaide, 1986

Hornadge, Bill, *Dubbo walkabout*, Review Publications, Dubbo, NSW, 1970

Jervis, James, *The Story of Parramatta and district*, Shakespeare Head Press, Sydney, 1933

Jounquay, Dorothy Agnes, *The Isisford story*, Isisford Shire Council, Isisford, Qld, 1975

Jones, M.A., *North Sydney 1788–1988*, Allen and Unwin, Sydney, 1988

Keating, Christopher, *Surry Hills, the city's backyard*, Hale & Iremonger, Sydney, 1991

Kelly, Max, *Paddock full of houses: Paddington 1840–1890*, Doak Press, Paddington, NSW, 1978

Kiernan, Brian (ed), *The essential Henry Lawson: The best works of Australia's greatest writer*, O'Neill, South Yarra, Vic, 1980

Larcombe, F.A., *Change & challenge: A history of the Municipality of Canterbury*, NSW, Canterbury Municipal Council, Canterbury, NSW, 1979

Larkins, John, *Australian pubs*, Rigby, Adelaide, 1973

Lea-Scarlett, Errol, *Queanbeyan: District and people*, Queanbeyan Municipal Council, Queanbeyan, NSW, 1968

Lee, Richard, *Country roads and bush pubs: The touring motorist's guide to rural Victoria*, Five Mile Press, Hawthorn, Vic, 1987

McCalman, Janet, *Struggletown: Portrait of an Australian working-class community*, Penguin, Ringwood, Vic, 1988

McDonald, Lorna, *Rockhampton: A history of city and district*, Rockhampton City Council, Rockhampton, Qld, 1995

McGoldrick, Prue, *When the whistle blew: A social history of the town of Sunshine 1920–1950*, Gippsland Printers (Morwell), Morwell, Vic, 1989

McGuire, Paul, *Inns of Australia*, Heinemann, Melbourne, 1952

Malone, Betty, *Prahran's pubs*, Prahran Bicentennial Community Committee in conjunction with the City of Prahran, Prahran, Vic, 1988

Morris, John, *Tall trees and tall tales: stories of old Pemberton*, Hesperian Press, Carlisle, WA, 1992

Moyes, John F., *A town called Port: A Port Macquarie-Hastings Valley walkabout*, Moyman Books, Port Macquarie, NSW, 1986

Mungindi and District Historical Society Book Committee, *A History of Mungindi to 1988*, Mungindi and District Historical Society Book Committee, Mungindi, NSW, 1988

Noye, Larry, *O'Malley, M.H.R*, Neptune Press, Geelong, Vic, 1985

O'Callaghan, Bill, *Wangaratta 1959–1984: A silver city*, City of Wangaratta, Wangaratta, 1984

O'Keefe, Daniel, *O'Keefe's guide to Sydney pubs*, Daniel O'Keefe Publications, Sydney, 1975

Parkes, W.S., *Mines, wines and people*, City of Greater Cessnock, Cessnock, NSW, 1979

Pullar, G.C., and Stringer, Marguerite, *A shifting town: Glass-plate images of Clermont and its people*, University of Queensland Press, St Lucia, Qld, 1986

Ramsland, John, *The struggle against isolation: A history of the Manning Valley*, Library of Australian History in association with Greater Taree City Council, North Sydney, NSW, 1987

Revitt, Jim, *The good old days along the Manning River and Great Lakes*, Anvil Press, Narara, NSW, 1979

Roberts, Ainslie, and Lockwood, Kim, *Darwin sketchbook*, Rigby, Adelaide, 1970

Roberts, Mick R., *The local: A history of hotels and the liquor industry in the far northern Illawarra of NSW*, M.R. Roberts, Bulli, NSW, 1992

Rolls, Eric C., *A million wild acres: 200 years of man and an Australian forest*, Melbourne, 1981

Royal Historical Society of Victoria, Bendigo Branch, *Historical guide to Bendigo including self tours of Bendigo's famous goldfields*, Royal Historical Society of Victoria, Bendigo Branch, Bendigo, Vic, 1968

Ryan, John L., *Before you came: Mines, myths & memories of Diamond Creek*, New Life Publications, Surrey Hills, Vic, 1972

Sheehy, Thomas, *Sandringham, a sketchbook history*, Victorian Society of Local History Writers, Bentleigh, Vic, 1972

Shield, Mark, *Daily Mirror guide to Sydney pubs*, McCulloch Publishing, Carlton, Vic, 1989

Shield, Mark, *The Advertiser guide to Adelaide pubs*, McCulloch Publishing, Carlton, Vic, 1989

Shield, Mark, *The Herald guide to Melbourne pubs*, McCulloch Publishing, Carlton, Vic, 1988

Stephens, Tony, and O'Neill, Annette, *Larrikin days: 100 years of growing up in an Australian suburb*, Nicholson Street Public School Parents & Citizens Association in association with John Fergusson, Balmain, NSW, 1983.

Symonds, Sally, *Healesville: History in the hills*, Pioneer Design Studio, Lilydale, Vic, 1982

Todd, Graham, *The Goondiwindi story*, Boolarong, Bowen Hills, Qld, 1988

Tulloch, David J., *100 years of Wentworth*, Wentworth Shire Council, Wentworth, NSW, 1959

Tuxworth, Hilda, *Tennant Creek yesterday and today*, H.Tuxworth, Tennant Creek, NT, 1978

Uren, Malcolm, *The City of Melville, from bushland to expanding metropolis*, Melville City Council, Ardross, WA, 1975

Von Stieglitz, K.R., *A history of New Norfolk and the Derwent Valley*, Evandale, Tas, 1961

Von Stieglitz, K.R., *A short history of Ross*, K.R. Von Stieglitz, Evandale, Tas, 1949

Von Stieglitz, K.R., *Longford past and present*, K.R. Von Stieglitz, Evandale, Tas, 1947

Wannan, Bill, *Bill Wannan's Australian bushranging: The stark story*, Rigby, Adelaide, 1978

Wapping History Group, *Down Wapping: Hobart's vanished Wapping and Old Wharf districts*, Blubber Head Press, Hobart, 1994

Ware, Syd H., *A history of Werris Creek and district: Tracing the discovery and early settlement of Weia Weia Creek Valley*, Quirindi and District Historical Society, Quirindi, NSW, 1976

Whitelaw, Ella, *A history of Singleton, Singleton Historical Society*, Singleton, NSW, 1971

Wilson, H.H., *The golden miles*, Rigby, Adelaide, 1977

Woodberry, Joan, and Woodberry, Frank, *Historic Hobart sketchbook*, Rigby, Adelaide, 1976

Index of pubs